Penguin Books

Use of Lateral Thinking

Edward de Bono was born in Malta and after his initial education at St Edward's College, Malta, and the Royal University of Malta, where he obtained a degree in medicine, he proceeded as a Rhodes Scholar to Christ Church, Oxford, where he gained an honours degree in psychology and physiology and then a D.Phil. in medicine. He also holds a Ph.D. from Cambridge. He has had faculty appointments at the universities of Oxford, London, Cambridge and Harvard.

Dr de Bono is the founder and director of the Cognitive Research Trust in Cambridge (founded 1969) and the Centre for the Study of Thinking, and a founder of SITO (Supranational Independent Thinking Organization). He runs what is now the largest curriculum programme in the world for the direct teaching of thinking in schools. Dr de Bono's instruction in thinking has been sought by many of the leading corporations such as IBM, Shell, Unilever, ICI, Du Pont, Monsanto, United Technologies and many others. He has been invited to lecture extensively throughout the world.

He has written twenty-five books which have been translated into twenty languages. He has also completed two TV series, 'The Greatest Thinkers' for WDR, Germany, and 'De Bono's Course in Thinking' for the BBC. Dr de Bono is the originator of the term 'lateral thinking' and also the inventor of the classic L-game, which is said to be the simplest real game ever invented. He is the author of *Letter to Thinkers*, which is published ten times a year.

His books include *The Five-Day Course in Thinking* (1968), *The Mechanism of Mind* (1969), *Lateral Thinking* (1970), *The Dog-Exercising Machine* (1970), *Technology Today* (1971), *Practical Thinking* (1971), *Lateral Thinking for Management* (1971), *Po: Beyond Yes and No* (1972), *Children Solve Problems* (1972), *Eureka!: An Illustrated History of Inventions from the Wheel to the Computer* (1974), *Teaching Thinking* (1976), *The Greatest Thinkers* (1976), *Wordpower* (1977), *The Happiness Purpose* (1977), *Future Positive* (1979), *Atlas of Management Thinking* (1981), *De Bono's Course in Thinking* (1982), *Tactics: The Art and Science of Success* (1985), *Conflicts: A Better Way to Resolve Them* and *Six Thinking Hats* (forthcoming). Many of these have been published in Penguin. Dr de Bono has also contributed to many journals, including the *Lancet* and *Clinical Science*. He is married and has two sons.

Edward de Bono

The Use of Lateral Thinking

Penguin Books

PENGUIN BOOKS

Published by the Penguin Group
Penguin Books Ltd, 27 Wrights Lane, London W8 5TZ, England
Viking Penguin, a division of Penguin Books USA Inc.
375 Hudson Street, New York, New York 10014, USA
Penguin Books Australia Ltd, Ringwood, Victoria, Australia
Penguin Books Canada Ltd, 2801 John Street, Markham, Ontario, Canada L3R 1B4
Penguin Books (NZ) Ltd, 182–190 Wairau Road, Auckland 10, New Zealand

Penguin Books Ltd, Registered Offices: Harmondsworth, Middlesex, England

First published by Jonathan Cape 1967
Published in Pelican Books 1971
Reprinted in Penguin Books 1990
10 9 8 7 6 5 4 3 2 1

Made and printed in Great Britain by
BPCC Hazell Books
Aylesbury, Bucks, England
Member of BPCC Ltd.
Set in Linotype Juliana

Foreword

Why do some people always seem to be having new ideas while others of equal intelligence never do?

Since Aristotle, logical thinking has been exalted as the one effective way in which to use the mind. Yet the very elusiveness of new ideas indicates that they do not necessarily come about as a result of logical thought processes. Some people are aware of another sort of thinking which is most easily recognized when it leads to those simple ideas that are obvious only after they have been thought of. This book is an attempt to look at this sort of thinking and to show that it is quite distinct from logic and often more useful in generating new ideas. For the sake of convenience, the term 'lateral thinking' has been coined to describe this other sort of thinking; 'vertical thinking' is used to denote the conventional logical process.

To trace fully what goes on in the mind, all its activity ultimately needs to be translated into patterns of excitation in the nerve networks of the brain. Relatively little is known at present about the detailed workings of the brain, yet it is possible to entertain a broad concept of its organization. Just as the functional organization of the electric circuit in a house may be appreciated without details of the layout of each wire or the design of each switch, so an understanding of thought processes may be approached by examining the outward manifestation of mind for evidence of underlying systems. A system analysis of this kind would consider, for example, the effects of a complex interaction of positive and negative feedback.

Such a view of brain function, however, serves only as a convenient model for the development of the concept of lateral thinking. Even so, the usefulness of lateral thinking does not in any way depend on the validity of the model. Supposing the model is valid, it would be as irrelevant to the skilful use of lateral thinking as a knowledge of engineering is to the skilful car driver. No one would suggest that the proper use of logical thinking has depended on a full understanding of the behaviour of the brain.

The notions expressed in this book, therefore, are based on simple observation and on a certain concept of the functional organization of the brain. Ordinary terms such as 'thoughts', 'ideas' and 'perceptions' are used, as these terms seem to make most sense in this context.

Lateral thinking is not a new, magic formula but simply a different and more creative way of using the mind. The New Maths makes good use of lateral thinking, the psychedelic cult is an abuse of it. The New Maths is specially apt as an example because, in place of the old fixed approach to mathematics, it substitutes a direct development of the pupil, giving him a more personal sense of achievement. This encourages much greater flexibility of mind, for the pupil is actively encouraged to consider a problem from many different points of view, and to appreciate that there may be several ways of reaching a correct conclusion. In time the same principles, which are all basic to lateral thinking, may come to permeate other fields of learning.

After reading this book some people will recognize lateral thinking as something that has been glimpsed tantalizingly now and then; occasions may be recalled when brilliant results have been obtained by using it. No textbook could be compiled to teach lateral thinking, although in the following pages it is suggested how certain techniques might be consciously applied to help break the stranglehold of logical thinking. The idea here is to show what lateral thinking is and how it works, and then to stimulate readers to develop their own potential for thinking in this manner.

1

Many years ago when a person who owed money could be thrown into jail, a merchant in London had the misfortune to owe a huge sum to a money-lender. The money-lender, who was old and ugly, fancied the merchant's beautiful teenage daughter. He proposed a bargain. He said he would cancel the merchant's debt if he could have the girl instead.

Both the merchant and his daughter were horrified at the proposal. So the cunning money-lender proposed that they let Providence decide the matter. He told them that he would put a black pebble and a white pebble into an empty money-bag and then the girl would have to pick out one of the pebbles. If she chose the black pebble she would become his wife and her father's debt would be cancelled. If she chose the white pebble she would stay with her father and the debt would still be cancelled. But if she refused to pick out a pebble her father would be thrown into jail and she would starve.

Reluctantly the merchant agreed. They were standing on a pebble-strewn path in the merchant's garden as they talked and the money-lender stooped down to pick up the two pebbles. As he picked up the pebbles the girl, sharp-eyed with fright, noticed that he picked up two black pebbles and put them into the money-bag. He then asked the girl to pick out the pebble that was to decide her fate and that of her father.

Imagine that you are standing on that path in the merchant's garden. What would you have done if you had been the unfortunate girl? If you had had to advise her what would you have advised her to do?

What type of thinking would you use to solve the problem? You may believe that careful logical analysis must solve the problem if there is a solution. This type of thinking is straightforward vertical thinking. The other type of thinking is lateral thinking.

Vertical thinkers are not usually of much help to a girl in this situation. The way they analyse it, there are three possibilities:

1. The girl should refuse to take a pebble.
2. The girl should show that there are two black pebbles in the bag and expose the money-lender as a cheat.
3. The girl should take a black pebble and sacrifice herself in order to save her father from prison.

None of the suggestions is very helpful, for if the girl does not take a pebble her father goes to prison, and if she does take a pebble, then she has to marry the money-lender.

The story shows the difference between vertical thinking and lateral thinking. Vertical thinkers are concerned with the fact that the girl has to take a pebble. Lateral thinkers become concerned with the pebble that is left behind. Vertical thinkers take the most reasonable view of a situation and then proceed logically and carefully to work it out. Lateral thinkers tend to explore all the different ways of looking at something, rather than accepting the most promising and proceeding from that.

The girl in the pebble story put her hand into the money-bag and drew out a pebble. Without looking at it she fumbled and let it fall to the path where it was immediately lost among all the others.

'Oh, how clumsy of me,' she said, 'but never mind – if you look into the bag you will be able to tell which pebble I took by the colour of the one that is left.'

Since the remaining pebble is of course black, it must be assumed that she has taken the white pebble, since the money-lender dare not admit his dishonesty. In this way, by using lateral thinking, the girl changes what seems an impossible situation into an extremely advantageous one. The girl is actually better off than if the money-lender had been honest and had put one black and one white pebble into the bag, for then she would have had only an even chance of being saved. As it is, she is sure of remaining with her father and at the same time having his debt cancelled.

Vertical thinking has always been the only respectable type of thinking. In its ultimate form as logic it is the recommended ideal towards which all minds are urged to strive, no matter how far short they fall. Computers are perhaps the best example. The problem is defined by the programmer, who also indicates the path along which the problem is to be explored. The computer then proceeds with its uncomparable logic and efficiency to work out the problem. The smooth progression of vertical thinking, from one solid step to another solid step is quite different from lateral thinking.

If you were to take a set of toy blocks and build them upwards, each block resting firmly and squarely on the block below it, you would have an illustration of vertical thinking. With lateral thinking the blocks are scattered around. They may be connected to each other loosely or not at all. But the pattern that may eventually emerge can be as useful as the vertical structure.

Lateral thinking is easiest to appreciate when it is seen in action, as in the pebble story. Everyone has come across the sort of problem which seems impossible to solve until suddenly a surprisingly simple solution is revealed. Once it has been thought of, the solution is so obvious that one cannot understand why it was ever so difficult to find. This sort of problem may indeed be difficult to solve so long as vertical thinking is used.

Lateral thinking is not only concerned with problem-solving; it has to do with new ways of looking at things and new ideas of every sort.

If a story like the pebble story is read straight through and the solution given immediately, then the listeners are inclined to wonder what the fuss is about. It is only if there is a pause for the listeners to find the solution for themselves that the difficulty of finding one is appreciated. With the best examples of lateral thinking the solution does seem logically obvious once it has been reached. It is very easy to forget that it has been reached by lateral thinking and not by vertical thinking. Once the solution has been revealed many people are prepared to explain how it could perfectly well have been reached by vertical thinking. In retrospect the logical sequence from the problem to its solution may be quite easy to see.

While in a trance a hypnotized person can be instructed to carry out some bizarre behaviour after emerging from the trance. When the time comes the subject duly carries out the hypnotist's instructions, which may have been to put up an umbrella in the drawing-room, to hand everyone a glass of milk, or to drop on all fours and bark like a dog. When asked why he is behaving in the odd way the subject immediately provides a perfectly reasonable explanation. Such an explanation offers an unforgettable demonstration of the powers of rationalization. Everyone present knows the real reason behind the odd behaviour and yet the person carrying it out can construct a perfectly reasonable explanation which would convince any late-comer.

There is no harm in rationalizing a vertical-thinking path to the solution after it has been reached by lateral thinking. The danger lies in assuming that because such a path can be constructed in retrospect, all problems can be solved as easily with vertical thinking as they might be with lateral thinking.

One of the techniques of lateral thinking is to make deliberate use of this rationalizing facility of the mind. Instead of proceeding step by step in the usual vertical manner, you take up a new and quite arbitrary position. You then work backwards and try to construct a logical path between this new position and the starting point. Should a path prove possible, it must eventually be tested with the full rigours of logic. If the path is sound, you are then in a useful position which may never have been reached by ordinary vertical thinking. Even if the arbitrary position does not prove tenable, you may still have generated useful new ideas in trying to justify it.

A few people come to like the idea of lateral thinking so much that they try to use it instead of vertical thinking on all occasions. Many more people resent the idea of lateral thinking and insist that vertical thinking is quite sufficient. In fact, the two types of thinking are complementary. When ordinary vertical thinking is unable to find a solution to a problem or when a new idea is required, then lateral thinking should be used. New ideas depend on lateral thinking, for vertical thinking has inbuilt limitations which make it much less effective for this purpose. These limitations of vertical thinking cannot be set aside, for they are its very advantages, looked at from a different point of view.

The functional organization of the mind as an optimizing system makes it interpret a situation in the most probable way. The order of probability is determined by experience and by the needs of the moment. Vertical thinking is high-probability thinking. Without such high-probability thinking, everyday life would be impossible. Every action and every sensation would have to be intensely analysed and carefully considered – nothing could ever be taken for granted. Like the centipede, confused by self-consciousness, everyone would be incapacitated by complexity. The function of thought is to eliminate itself and allow action to follow directly on recognition of a situation. This is only possible if the most probable interpretation of a situation gives rise to the most probably effective action.

Just as water flows down slopes, settles in hollows and is confined to riverbeds, so vertical thinking flows along the most probable paths and by its very flow increases the probability of those paths for the future. If vertical thinking is high-probability thinking, then lateral thinking is low-probability thinking. New channels are deliberately cut to alter the flow of the water. The old channels are dammed up in the hope that the water will seek out and take to new and better patterns of flow. Sometimes the water is even sucked upwards in an unnatural fashion. When the low-probability line of thought leads to an effective new idea there is a 'eureka moment', and at once the low-probability approach acquires the highest probability. It is the moment when the water sucked upward with difficulty forms a siphon and at once flows freely. This moment is always the aim of lateral thinking.

Since lateral thinking is to do with new ideas it would seem to be related to creative thinking. Creative thinking is a special part of lateral thinking which covers a wider field. Sometimes the achievements of lateral thinking are genuine creations, at other times they are nothing more than a new way of looking at things, and hence somewhat less than full creations. Creative thinking often requires a talent for expression, whereas lateral thinking is open to everyone who is interested in new ideas.

In this book creative thinking in the true artistic sense has not been used as an example of lateral thinking because the outcome is too subjective. It is easy to demonstrate the effectiveness of lateral thinking with an invention, which either works or does not. It is also easy to decide whether a problem has been effectively solved with lateral thinking. But the value of artistic creative effort is a matter of taste and of fashion.

The further lateral thinking diverges from the rules of

reason and vertical thinking, the more it must seem to approach madness. Is lateral thinking only a form of deliberate and temporary madness? Is low-probability thinking any different from the random associations of the schizophrenic? One of the most characteristic features of schizophrenia is the butterfly mind which flies from idea to idea. If one wants to escape temporarily from the obvious way of looking at things, why not use a psychedelic drug? The essential difference is that with lateral thinking the whole process is firmly controlled. If lateral thinking chooses to use chaos it is chaos by direction, not chaos through absence of direction. All the time the logical faculty is waiting to elaborate and eventually judge and select whatever new ideas are generated. The difference between lateral and vertical thinking is that with vertical thinking logic is in control of the mind, whereas with lateral thinking logic is at the service of the mind.

Does a person have a fixed skill in thinking or only as much ability as he has had interest and opportunity to develop? Only a few people have a natural aptitude for lateral thinking, but everyone can develop a certain skill if they set about it deliberately. Orthodox education usually does nothing to encourage lateral thinking habits and positively inhibits them with the need to conform one's way through the successive examination hoops.

Lateral thinking is not a magic formula which can be learned at once and usefully applied thereafter. It is an attitude and a habit of mind. The various techniques described are intended to bring about an awareness of lateral-thinking processes; they are not meant to be used as a problem-solving cook-book. There is no sudden conversion from a belief in the omnipotence of vertical thinking to a belief in the usefulness of lateral thinking. Lateral thinking is a matter of awareness and practice – not revelation.

2

How many people will have a single new idea in the course of their lives? How many people would be capable of inventing the wheel if it had not been invented?

Many find that new ideas, like accidents, always happen to other people. The supposition is that the other people are better qualified to have new ideas and also have more opportunity.

It would be much more satisfactory if new ideas were the just reward for hard work and persistent effort. There are many people who certainly work hard enough to deserve new ideas, and it would be most fitting if their good will and sacrifice culminated in a new idea. Society would also feel much happier encouraging, organizing and recognizing the solid effort behind new ideas if they could be brought about in this way.

Unfortunately new ideas are not the prerogative of those who spend a long time seeking and developing them. Charles Darwin spent more than twenty years working on his theory of evolution, and then one day he was asked to read over a paper by a young biologist called Alfred Russell Wallace. Ironically the paper contained a clear exposition of the theory of evolution by survival of the fittest. It seems that Wallace had worked out the theory in one week of delirium in the East Indies. The full development of an idea may well take years of hard work but the idea itself may arrive in a flash of insight. In fact, when the idea involves a completely new way of looking at things it is hard to see how a new idea could come about in any other way. The new idea does not have to be preceded by years of work in the field, for dissatisfaction with the old idea may happen much more quickly than that. Indeed, such years of work may even make new ideas more hard to come by, since over the years the usefulness of the old ideas may be reinforced if they have any usefulness at all. The scientific world is full of hard-working scientists who lack nothing as regards the logic of their approach and the meticulousness of their work, yet new ideas may for ever elude them.

A great many new ideas come about when new information gathered by observation or experiment forces a reappraisal of the old ideas. New information is probably the surest road to new ideas, but it is still unreliable, for mostly the new information is explained by the old theory and fashioned to support that theory. A patient who is being treated by a psychoanalyst may well find that any new symptoms he dreams up is ably interpreted as supporting the analyst's established diagnosis. Indeed, many feel that the longevity of Freud's theories is partly explained by their resilience in accommodating any experimental evidence offered to refute them.

Although new information can lead to new ideas, these can also come about without any new information at all. It is perfectly possible to look at all the old information and come up with a very worthwhile new way of putting it together. The most perfect example of this is, of course, Einstein. Einstein did no experiments, gathered no new information, before he created the theory of relativity. Since he did no experiments he contributed nothing except a new way of looking at information that had been available to everyone else. The experiments confirming the theory came afterwards. What Einstein did was to look at all the existing information which everyone else was content to fit into the Newtonian structure, and to put it together in a completely new way. It is frightening (or exciting) to contemplate how many new ideas are lying dormant in already collected information that is now put together in one way and could be rearranged in a better way. At first Einstein's theories were only minimally more adequate than the ones they replaced. The difference in explanation amounted to a better understanding of the wavelengths of light from the star Sirius and a very slight alteration in the orbit of the planet Mercury. In terms of detail this was like replacing a cup in a restaurant, but from that new way of looking at things came atomic energy.

When they think of new ideas many people think of technical inventions or scientific theories. In both instances the appropriate technical knowledge seems to be required before any new ideas are possible. This is perfectly true, but clearly technical knowledge is not enough, for even the people who possess it do not automatically come up with new ideas. One American woman made a fortune from figuring out how to fold a piece of paper so that it could be used as a payment slip, a bill and a receipt. It saved so much time and effort and stationery that it became widely adopted. The process by which new ideas come about can be separated from the actual importance of those ideas. Even trivial new ideas can come about in the same way as those ideas that change the course of history. It is said that the great Napoleon found it just as difficult to get rid of his wife's dog as he did to get rid of the powerful armies sent against him.

A very good instance of how technical knowledge and the right setting are not sufficient to bring about a new idea is to be found in the story of the thermionic valve – an invention on which was based the whole development of electronic technology, with its wonders of communication. Edison, the electricity wizard, actually held in his hands a device like an electric light bulb which we can now recognize as a primitive form of the thermionic valve. He did more than just hold it in his hands, he even took out a patent on it. No one could have been in a better position to appreciate the significance of the device than Edison, no one could have had a better background in the field of electricity. But it was years later that the significance of the device was realized by Fleming in London, and then Lee De Forest went on to develop the triode valve – though even he did not appreciate its full value until telephone engineers began to find it useful.

The defeatist explanation for the extraordinary elusiveness of new ideas is that they are a matter of chance. According to this theory a new idea cannot come about until the basic ingredients are brought together at one time, in a special way, in the mind of one man. It becomes a matter of waiting until chance brings about this fertile assembly of information. This is a very negative approach, yet there is much evidence to support it.

The mind of man has shown great vigour and efficiency in developing ideas once they have come about. In the course of a single life-time the aeroplane has developed from a daring experiment by two bicycle mechanics to the most effective form of transport, whose convenience and efficiency are taken for granted. The radio has developed from a fragile miracle to a cheap commonplace. Development is something at which the mind excels: there are no conceivable limits to its excellence in this direction, which extends to the design of auxiliary electronic minds that can carry its developing capacity even farther. In contrast to this facility for development, the ability to generate fundamentally new ideas is poor. New ideas come about only sporadically even when the technology which makes them possible has been available for a long time. A Hovercraft could have been constructed long before Christopher Cockerell came up with this new idea. The availability of technology does, however, make feasible ideas which would otherwise be abandoned. For instance, Charles Babbage, the

Lucasian professor of mathematics at Cambridge, would certainly have set about constructing the first computer in the 1830s had he not been frustrated by the lack of electronic technology which eventually made computers possible. His ideas were sound, but he was confined to mechanical cogs. But technology by itself does not generate new ideas.

If one accepts the passive approach to new ideas, then there is nothing that can be done except to wait, hope and pray. There is, however, an alternative approach. If new ideas are entirely a matter of chance, then how is it that some people, like Edison, have so very many more new ideas than other people? Inventors and famous scientists usually produce a string of new ideas, not just one. This suggests that there is a capacity for generating new ideas that is better developed in some people than in others. This capacity does not seem to be related to sheer intelligence but more to a particular habit of mind, a particular way of thinking.

The rewards of new ideas may be very considerable or they may be very meagre. The man who invented the combine harvester made a fortune, the men who invented the first sewing machine did not. The only reward that can be relied upon is the pleasure of achievement. This is quite different from the pleasure that attends other forms of achievement: it is an excitement in a higher key.

Once a new idea springs into existence it cannot be unthought. There is a sense of immortality in a new idea.

3

It is one thing to suggest that new ideas are useful, profitable and exciting, but quite another thing to suggest that something deliberate can be done about having new ideas. No one would disagree with the first suggestion, but most would doubt the second.

There are two opposite ways of improving a process. The first way is to try to improve it directly. The second is to recognize, and then remove, those influences that inhibit the process. If a car does not seem to be moving fast enough the driver may either press harder on the accelerator or he may make sure the brake has been fully released. To design a car that goes faster the designer could either put in a more powerful engine, or reduce the weight and air resistance which slow the car down.

It may be more useful to study stupidity in order to understand intelligence. It may be easier to see what the stupid person lacks than to see what the clever person has extra. Instead of trying to understand why one person invents, it may make more sense to see why other people do not. If it is possible to obtain some insight into what prevents the emergence of new ideas, either in general or in a particular person, then it may be possible to improve the ability to have new ideas.

Lateral thinking is made necessary by the limitations of

vertical thinking. The terms 'lateral' and 'vertical' were suggested by the following considerations.

It is not possible to dig a hole in a different place by digging the same hole deeper.

Logic is the tool that is used to dig holes deeper and bigger, to make them altogether better holes. But if the hole is in the wrong place, then no amount of improvement is going to put it in the right place. No matter how obvious this may seem to every digger, it is still easier to go on digging in the same hole than to start all over again in a new place. Vertical thinking is digging the same hole deeper; lateral thinking is trying again elsewhere.

The disinclination to abandon a half-dug hole is partly a reluctance to abandon the investment of effort that has gone into the hole without seeing some return. It is also easier to go on doing the same thing rather than wonder what else to do: there is a strong practical commitment to it.

It is not possible to look in a different direction by looking harder in the same direction. No sooner are two thoughts strung together than there is a direction, and it becomes easier to string further thoughts along in the same direction than to ignore it. Ignoring something can be hard work, especially if there is not yet an alternative.

These two sorts of commitments to the half-dug hole may be regarded as commitment of invested effort and commitment of direction.

By far the greatest amount of scientific effort is directed towards the logical enlargement of some accepted hole. Many are the minds scratching feebly away or gouging out great chunks according to their capacity. Yet great new ideas and great scientific advances have often come about through people ignoring the hole that is in progress and starting a new one. The reason for starting a new one could be dissatisfaction with the old one, sheer ignorance of the old one, a temperamental need to be different, or pure whim. This hole-hopping is rare, because the process of education is usually effective and education is designed to make people appreciate the holes that have been dug for them by their betters. Education could only lead to chaos if it were to do otherwise. Adequacy and competence could hardly be built on the encouragement of general dissatisfaction with the existing array of holes. Nor is education really concerned with progress: its purpose is to make widely available knowledge that seems to be useful. It is communicative, not creative.

To accept the old holes and then ignore them and start again is not as easy as being unaware of them and hence free to start anywhere. Many great discoverers like Faraday had no formal education at all, and others, like Darwin or Clerk Maxwell, had insufficient to curb their originality. It is tempting to suppose that a capable mind that is unaware of the old approach has a good chance of evolving a new one.

A half-dug hole offers a direction in which to expend effort. Effort needs a direction and there are few more frustrating things than eager effort looking for a direction. Effort must also be rewarded by some tangible result; the more immediate the results, the more encouraged is the effort. Enlarging the hole that is being dug offers real progress and an assurance of future achievement. Finally, there is a comfortable, earned familiarity with a well-worked hole.

To abandon a sizeable hole without any idea as to where a new hole ought to be started is unreasonable and demands too much of practical human nature. It is difficult enough even when a site has been chosen for the new hole.

Oilmen do not perhaps find it so difficult to appreciate the paradox that sitting about deciding where to dig another hole may be more useful than digging the same hole deeper. Perhaps the difference is that, for an oilman, digging costs money, but for scientists and industrialists, not digging is more expensive. Without a hole, how can the mind exert its well-trained effort? The shovels of logic lie idle. There is no progress, no achievement. Today achievement has come to be ever more important to the scientist. It is by achievement alone that effort is judged, and to pursue his career a scientist must survive many such judgements.

No one is paid to sit around being capable of achievement. As there is no way of assessing such capability it is necessary to pay and promote according to visible achievements. Far better to dig the wrong hole (even one that is recognized as being wrong) to an impressive depth than to sit around wondering where to start digging. It may well be that the person who is sitting around and thinking is far closer to digging a much more valuable hole, but how can such a thing be judged until the hole is actually started and the achievement becomes visible?

In the long run it may be far more useful to have some people about to achieve the right thing than have everyone actually achieving things of lesser worth, but there are few who are willing to invest in mere possibility. In the present system who can afford to think? Who can afford the non-progress of abortive thought?

An expert is an expert because he understands the present hole better than anyone else except a fellow expert, with whom it is necessary to disagree in order that there can be as many experts as there are disagreements – for among the experts a hierarchy can then emerge. An expert may even have contributed towards the shape of the hole. For such reasons experts are not usually the first to leap out of the hole that accords them their expert status, to start digging elsewhere. It would be even more unthinkable for an expert to climb out of the hole only to sit around and consider where to start another hole. Nor are experts eager to express their expertise as dissatisfaction with the hole, for dissatisfaction is too easily expressed, and often more forcibly, by many others who have not earned the right to be dissatisfied. So experts are usually to be found happily at the bottom of the deepest holes, often so deep that it hardly seems worth getting out of them to look around.

Because the mind is happier enlarging by logic an existing hole; because education has encouraged this; and because society has elected experts to see that it is done, there are a lot of well-developed holes continually enlarging under the impact of logical effort. Many of the holes are extremely valuable in terms of the ore of practical knowledge that is removed from them. Others are a waste of effort.

There is nothing wrong with a hole that is a waste of effort. At least there is nothing wrong with its location, though the size may be extravagant. There ought to be many more such holes in original places. Many of them might well be a waste of effort, but some of them could turn out to be extremely useful. But to start such holes more people would have to escape the powerful commitment there is to the dominant hole.

The effect of the dominance of old and apparently adequate ideas is often underestimated. It is assumed that an old idea should be regarded as a useful stepping stone to something better until that something better turns up. This policy may be practical but it can inhibit the emergence of new ideas. If a good cartoonist has captured with a few dominant lines the impression of a face, it is extremely difficult to put that impression aside, look at the face again and come up with a new way of expressing it.

Sects which assemble on mountain tops on predicted days of doom to await the end of the world do not come down on the morrow shaken in their ideas, but with a renewed faith in the mercifulness of the Almighty. New information which could lead to the destruction of an old idea is readily incorporated into it instead, for the more information that can be accommodated, the sounder the idea becomes. It is like putting some drops of quicksilver on a surface. If you make one drop larger and larger, it approaches the neighbouring drops, and as soon as it touches them they lose their identity and become shifted bodily into the larger drop. As with dominant ideas, the big drop always swallows up the smaller one; it is not a matter of compromise.

An extreme example of the effect of dominant ideas is provided by the mental illness known as paranoia. Paranoia is fascinating because the logical reasoning powers of the mind are not impaired as they might be in other forms of mental illness. Sometimes the power of reason even seems to be more acute. The only abnormality is that the patient is dominated by the idea that he is being persecuted. Everything that happens, however trivial or remote, is interpreted as being directed at the patient. Kindness to the patient is regarded as a sinister attempt to gain his confidence in order to destroy him. Food is assumed to be poisoned. Newspapers are found to be full of coded threats. There is nothing that cannot be interpreted in this manner.

Dominant ideas need not always be so obvious for them to exert just as powerful an organizing influence on the way a person thinks and approaches a problem. Old and adequate ideas, like old and adequate cities, come to polarize everything around them. All organization is based on them, all things are referred to them. Minor alterations can be made on the outskirts, but it is impossible to change the whole structure radically and very difficult to shift the centre of organization to a different place.

How does one escape from the influence of such dominating ideas? A useful technique of lateral thinking is to pick out very deliberately, to define and even write down the idea that seems to be dominating the situation. Once an idea has been exposed in this way it becomes easier to recognize and therefore avoid its polarizing influence. It seems obvious and easy to do, but the exposure must be careful and deliberate; a general vague consciousness of the dominant idea is of no use at all.

Another technique is to acknowledge the dominant idea and then gradually distort it until in the end it loses its identity and collapses. The distortion may simply involve carrying the idea to extremes, or it may involve the exaggeration of only one feature. Once again, the process must be quite deliberate and self-conscious.

It might seem easier to identify the dominant idea and then vigorously to reject it. But rejection is only exchanging positive domination for negative domination, and instead of weakening the dominant idea it may even strengthen it. Moreover, freedom of thought is just as limited by rejection of an idea as by acceptance of that idea. This situation in a mild form is often to be found in young students who read a lot of philosophy. They find themselves in the awkward position of either having to agree with what they read, or else to disagree violently. Either way the simple awareness of a particular idea may inhibit the formation of an original idea in a mind capable of original ideas.

It may be better to read nothing and to run the risk of coming up with ideas that have already been proposed, than to be so aware of such ideas that no ideas of one's own can develop. Where a new idea unwittingly overlaps an old idea, then prior knowledge of the old idea may well distort or inhibit the new one. The views of a good teacher are often echoed down the years in approval or disapproval by his students whose own capacity for ideas is thereby impaired.

More often the danger is not one of over-awareness of an idea, but of neglect of ways of looking at things that are blotted out by a dominant idea. The story of the jumping spider illustrates this in a macabre fashion. The schoolboy had an interesting theory: he maintained that spiders could hear with their legs and he said that he could prove this.

He placed the spider in the middle of the table and said, 'Jump!' The spider jumped. The boy repeated the demonstration. Then he cut off the spider's legs and put it back in the middle of the table. Again he said, 'Jump!' But this time the spider remained quite still.

'See,' said the boy, 'you cut off a spider's legs and it goes stone deaf.'

Every scientist has heard this story and many honest ones can remember instances from their own experience when they were completely oblivious to other ways of looking at their experimental results, so dominated were they by their own theory. Not only is one's own theory very reasonable, but it is also one's own. Scientists have been pushed to extraordinary lengths through being dominated by proprietary interest in their own idea. The phenomenon is not restricted to the world of science.

It may be so difficult to escape from a dominant idea that it becomes impossible without outside help. It happens all the time in medicine when one doctor, too close to the patient's illness, tries hard to fit things into a certain diagnosis, and then another doctor comes along and with a fresh look at all the information offers a better and different diagnosis. In many closed communities, be they scientific or industrial, ideas tend to get very inbred. An outsider who can offer a fresh point of view may stimulate new ideas.

Having mentioned domination by zeal in the pursuit of one's own idea, domination through laziness must be mentioned also. It is much easier to accept an organizing idea that makes sense than to question that idea and have to go to the bother of making sense for oneself. Whoever offers packaged information (radio, television and the printed word) has the right, perhaps even the duty, to arrange that material in a presentable manner, and that implies some dominant theme. It is only too easy to accept the neatly organized packages that result. For this reason the wealth of new information that is made available by the media mentioned above very rarely gives rise to new ideas in the audience who, through laziness, remain dominated by the idea of those who present the information. Sometimes the dominant idea is obvious to everyone except oneself.

To cultivate a pleasure in being wrong sounds perverse, yet losing an argument means escaping from an old idea and the acquisition of a new way of looking at things. Being right usually adds only to one's self-esteem, though sometimes ideas do improve while they are being defended. The person who accepts an idea that is new for him may well do more with that idea than the person it came from, who may well have come to the end of his ability to develop it. Even if the new idea is discarded fairly soon, the disruption of the old idea may be worth the trouble of losing an argument honestly.

Probably the best caricature of the vertical thinker who becomes dominated by an idea is provided by the man whose cat had a kitten. Tired of letting the original cat in and out, he had hit on the idea of cutting a hole in the door so that the cat could come and go as it pleased without bothering him. As soon as the kitten arrived he at once cut a second, smaller hole in the door.

In Chapter 1, vertical thinking was compared to water which always flows into the most probable places. Using the same analogy, a dominant idea may be compared to a river that has cut deep into the land. The water which might have settled on the land is drained off so fast that there is no opportunity for lakes or other rivers to form. To realize that a dominant idea can be an obstacle instead of a convenience is the first principle of lateral thinking.

4

In writing about thinking it is easy to get lost in a confusion of unreal words and ideas. This chapter is an attempt to provide some tangible experience of the use of lateral thinking. General thought processes are directly translated into visual terms that provide a context for the exercise of lateral thinking. The visual involvement in the figures used provides a practical experience that gives substance to the more abstract descriptions used elsewhere.

That part of the world which forms the immediate environment could be called a situation. Another way of looking at it would be to consider a situation as including all that was accessible to immediate attention. At any moment attention may be directed to only one part of the situation. The result of such attention is a perception. The perception consists of information obtained by any number of different senses from that part of the environment which is being attended to. All the senses may contribute to the perception, but one of them alone would be sufficient.

Picture 1 on page 31 is a simple visual situation in black on white. It is simple enough to be attended to as a whole and hence is dealt with as a single perception. This perception makes use only of vision.

The simplicity of the situation and the fact that perception is entirely visual make the mental processes easier to observe, but will allow the situation to be representative of other

1

more complex situations which may require use of more senses than one.

The visual situation takes the form of a figure which is simple yet unfamiliar. It is unfamiliar in the sense that it has no definite name. No single word can be used to describe it in the way a square or hexagon or cross might be described.

The figure is so simple that a straightforward appreciation may seem all that is possible. There does not seem to be anything about it to understand or explain.

Throughout the exercise the need to understand a figure is replaced by the need to describe the figure to someone who cannot see it. This describing of a situation to another is similar to describing it to oneself, which is the process of understanding it.

The need for action is the most compelling reason for understanding a situation. In these examples the action required is that of describing the figure to someone else.

Since no single word in common use will describe the figure, and since familiar words are the only method of communication allowed, an attempt must be made to apply familiar words to an unfamiliar figure.

The figure can be understood only in terms of what is already familiar. The figure may be compared to some large familiar figure and the difference described. A more common method is to divide up the unfamiliar figure into familiar parts and then describe these and the way they come together to form the figure.

Picture 2 (page 33) shows one way in which the original figure can be broken down. Descriptions making use of this division of the original figure might run as follows:

1. Two parallel bars separated by two shorter cross-pieces inset from the ends of the bars.
2. A horizontal slab supported above an equal horizontal slab by two vertical pillars.

2

3. A rectangle with the two shorter ends pushed halfway towards the centre.

There are many other ways of describing this particular division. The division is purely a mental one, and once the pieces and their relationships have been transferred by description, then the listener tries to reassemble the complete figure. It is rather like transporting a cumbersome piece of machinery by taking it apart and sending assembly instructions along with the smaller, more convenient pieces.

The division shown in picture 2 (page 32) is quite arbitrary. Another way of dividing up the figure is shown in picture 3 (page 35). This could lead to a description somewhat as follows: two gutter-shaped pieces standing on edge and separated by two cross-pieces at the top and the bottom, the whole thing forming a single structure of uniform width.

Picture 4 at the bottom of page 35 is yet another division. This might be described as two interlocking 'L' pieces arranged to enclose a rectangle with two small bars continuing the longer arms of the 'L' pieces. Such a description is rather cumbersome and open to misunderstanding. It would only be used if the observer was very familiar with the 'L' pattern. The description of any situation depends on the familiar terms in which the observer wishes to describe it, and not on the best possible description.

The pieces created for the sake of explanation or description soon come to exist on their own as separate entities. They continue to exist even when the situation out of which they arose has been forgotten. The more useful the pieces prove to be for the explanation of other situations, the more assured is their survival.

In this way, entities which have been created quite arbitrarily become strengthened by their usefulness until it becomes impossible to doubt their existence. When this stage is reached such entities may actually obstruct progress. To

3

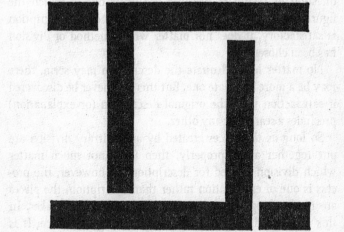

4

avoid this, the arbitrary nature of many entities must be kept in mind and none should be allowed to outlast its usefulness, since this is its only right to exist.

Picture 5 at the top of page 37 shows yet another way in which the original figure can be divided up. This division seems to result in more familiar elements than any previous division. Yet describing the relationships of the elements so that they can be reassembled into the complete figure will be found more difficult. It is not sufficient for an explanation to be a list of the most familiar elements available: the familiarity of the relationships must also be taken into account. Often use of the most familiar elements involves the least familiar relationships. A balance is necessary between familiarity of the elements and that of the relationships involved.

The division of an unfamiliar figure into familiar elements is always a matter of personal choice. The familiar elements are arbitrarily extracted from the original figure. There is no question of trying to discover the units out of which the figure may have been constructed. Provided the description is satisfactory, it does not matter which method of division has been chosen.

No matter how adequate the description may seem, there may be a more adequate one. But this will never be discovered if satisfaction with the original description (or explanation) precludes a search for any other.

So long as the pieces created by an arbitrary division are put together again properly, then it cannot much matter which division is used for description. If, however, the process is one of explanation rather than description, the pieces are not put together but examined for their own sakes. In this case the division used can make a big difference. It is quickly forgotten that the pieces have been arbitrarily created for the purpose of understanding the situation. Before being created in this manner the pieces do not exist as such, yet it is easy to believe that the situation is actually built up out of

5

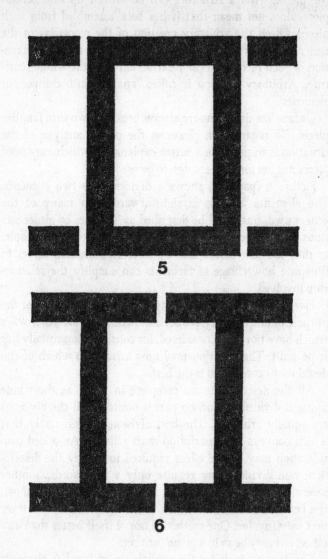

6

the pieces. That a structure can be broken up into certain pieces does not mean that it has been assembled from such pieces. Often the arbitrary creation of the pieces (as in the case of the figure shown here) is mistaken for a clever perception of such pieces and their extraction from the whole structure. Arbitrary division is called 'analysis into component elements'.

Unfamiliar situations are always broken down into familiar pieces. To regard such pieces as the proper analysis of the situation is to preclude a better explanation which may need pieces not yet familiar enough to be used.

Picture 6 (page 37) shows a division into two elements. The elements are less straightforward than many of the others used, but could be described as 'I' pieces or girder sections. The relationship between the pieces is extremely simple, as they are just placed side by side. This division serves to illustrate how choice of elements can simplify the relationship involved.

Five different ways of dividing up the original figure for the purpose of description have been shown. There are other ways which have not been considered, for consideration usually has some limit. The question may now arise as to which of the descriptions considered is the best.

All the descriptions are complete in so far as the whole figure is divided up and no part is omitted. All the divisions are equally arbitrary. The best division is presumably that which conveys the description most reliably. An added consideration may be the effort required to convey the description; one division may require only a few words, another several sentences, even if both are equally reliable. In short, the best division is that which is the most useful, whatever that may involve. One method is not of itself better than any other, but may be so in a given context.

The context includes the availability of familiar elements and relationships to whoever is making the description. The context also includes the availability (or an estimation of this) of these elements and relationships in the mind of the person for whom the description is intended. For instance, if the figure is being described to an engineer, then picture 6 may show the best way, as the term 'girder section' would be easily understood. The very arbitrariness of the division process allows a division to be deliberately suited to the understanding of the listener.

If the original figure as shown in picture 1 (page 31) is encountered often enough, it will become familiar and the need to divide it up into familiar elements will disappear. The figure may become so familiar that it may, itself, be useful for describing further unfamiliar situations.

In this way the repertoire of familiar figures and relationships is always growing. Once the process has been started, it feeds on itself, as unfamiliar figures explained by already familiar figures become familiar enough to explain further unfamiliar figures.

To become familiar, a figure must be encountered many times, and each time some behaviour associated with the figure must be repeated if the figure is to acquire a meaning.

In any large continuous pattern there may be some parts which seem separable from the whole. There may be lines of division which suggest themselves.

On pages 40 and 41 are shown four separate figures, which are simple but not simple enough to be described by a single word. The figures are very different, yet they can provide a single familiar figure.

Picture 8 (page 40) seems to offer natural lines of division into smaller elements. The 'T' shape can be taken off the top and the base can then be split into two other 'T' units.

If picture 7 is now considered in the light of what has been done to picture 8, it becomes obvious that the same 'T' unit will do as a basis of division.

For these limited circumstances the 'T' unit is becoming

7

8

9

10

increasingly familiar – so familiar that an attempt is made to describe pictures 9 and 10 in terms of the 'T' units.

While pictures 7 and 8 may have naturally fallen apart into 'T' units, the same could not be said of pictures 9 and 10. Had picture 10 been the first one examined, then the 'T' unit might never have grown into such a familiar figure.

On pages 43 and 44 are shown the divisions of each of the figures into arrangements of the simple 'T' unit.

In the above manner a familiar figure has come about by direct perception rather than through explanation by already familiar figures. Once this sort of start has been made, the whole expanding growth of familiar figures can proceed.

The creation of the 'T' unit has been quite arbitrary, even if picture 8 does suggest such a division. Once created, the 'T' unit proves itself by its usefulness in explaining the other figures on pages 43 and 44. This mobility and usefulness of the 'T' unit give it an existence of its own.

Nevertheless, the fact remains that no matter how conveniently figures may be divided into 'T' units, it cannot be said that they have been assembled out of 'T' units.

Had some other way been chosen for dividing up picture 8 (page 40), then such a way might have been perfectly adequate for describing this particular picture, but of no use in providing units for explaining the other pictures. It would have been adequate to describe picture 8 as consisting of a horizontal bar supported in the centre by a shorter vertical pillar resting on a larger horizontal bar which is in turn supported by two further vertical pillars inset from its ends. This description is just as adequate as the 'T' division. Thus though one description may be apparently no more adequate than another, its usefulness in general terms may be very different indeed. To allow satisfaction with the adequacy of an explanation to preclude search for other explanations is to reject progress.

Suppose the horizontal and vertical bar description of

11

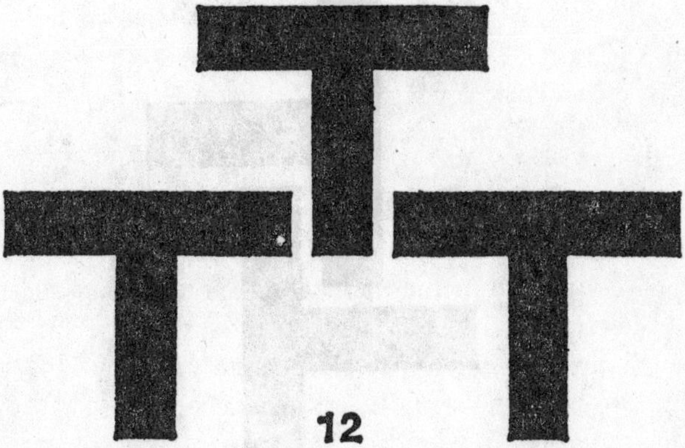

12

13

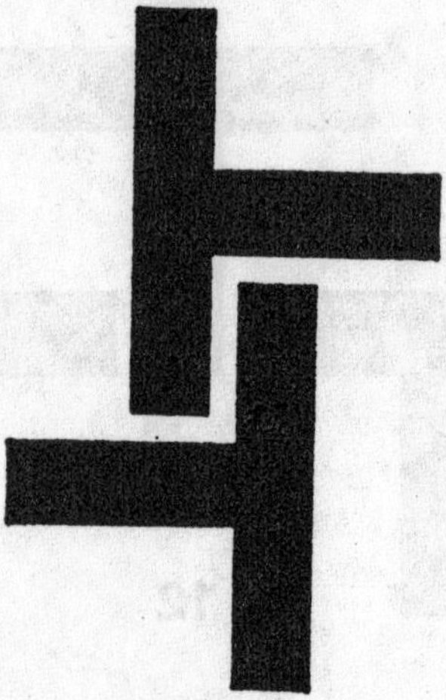

14

picture 8 had indeed been chosen and then examination of picture 7 had suggested a 'T' unit. Many people might have simply accepted this and gone their way. Others would have gone back to picture 8 and tried to see if the 'T' unit could also have been used there. This may seem the obvious thing to do, but it is neither obvious nor the usual way to behave. How many people deliberately try to reinterpret in the light of new information matters that already have an adequate explanation? Why should the 'T' unit arising out of one division seem useful enough to try out instead of the other explanation of picture 8? The 'T' unit comes to acquire importance with each successful application, but in the beginning it is no more important than any other element created by division of a figure. How many people would disregard an original adequate explanation for one which is no more adequate?

Those who are in the habit of performing such reinterpretations will not be surprised to find on page 46 a reinterpretation of the original figure in terms of the newly discovered 'T' unit.

A further point arises from this reinterpretation (picture 16, page 46). Had the original figure as reproduced in picture 15 been shown only after the 'T' unit had become familiar, then the figure would at once have been broken up into 'T' units. Another division would not have been considered, and might even have been resisted. It is only too easy to forget that no matter how adequate, the 'T' division is a personal and arbitrary matter and cannot exclude other descriptions (or explanations) which may be even more useful.

Because of the increasing familiarity of the 'T' unit, the temptation to regard division into such units as more valid than other divisions is strong. The 'T' unit is strengthened each time it is successfully used in a description. The more useful it appears, the more it comes to be used, and the more it is used the more useful it seems.

15

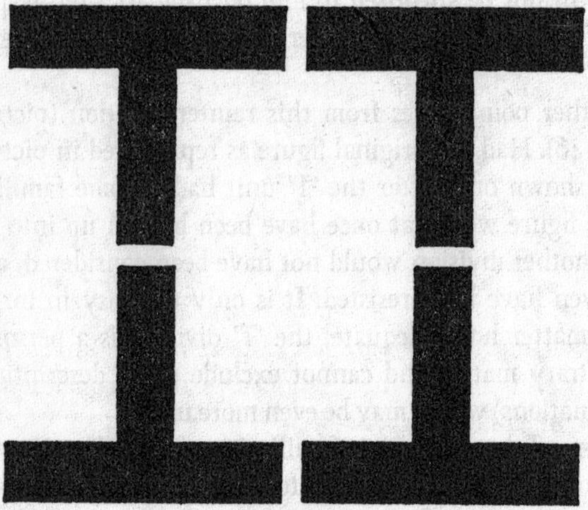

16

The mobility and usefulness of the 'T' unit lead to different figures being regarded as different arrangements of the basic unit. Each different figure provides a distinct pattern of relationships between 'T' units. These relationships may seem to have been discovered in the figure, but they are created by the determination to look at the figure in the 'T' way. Although the basic 'T' unit does not change, its constant use builds up a repertoire of different relationships. Unfamiliar figures that have become familiar through 'T' analysis also accumulate.

Picture 17 on page 48 is a complex enough figure and one that certainly requires breaking down into familiar elements if it is to be described. The resolution of the figure into 'T's is far from straightforward. If, however, the 'T' unit is the only available familiar unit, then an attempted description in these terms is essential, no matter how difficult.

Picture 18 (page 49) shows the successful division. The division is complete. This completeness may seem to justify the division. Nevertheless the division remains an arbitrary one. The availability of familiar figures is a personal matter and a limited supply cannot impose on a figure a limit to the ways in which it can be described by others who have a different supply.

If an attempt is made to describe picture 17 to someone else on the basis of the 'T' division shown in picture 18, it soon becomes apparent that the many relationships defining the positions of the 'T' pieces are not easy to handle. Though the 'T' unit itself is simple, the relationships are so complex that description is almost impossible.

Picture 19 (page 51) is a much simpler figure than picture 17, but it is still fairly complicated. Description in the 'T' manner can be attempted and once again this proves possible. The relationships between the various 'T' units in the descriptive division are, however, complicated.

Description becomes easier if the figure is divided not into

17

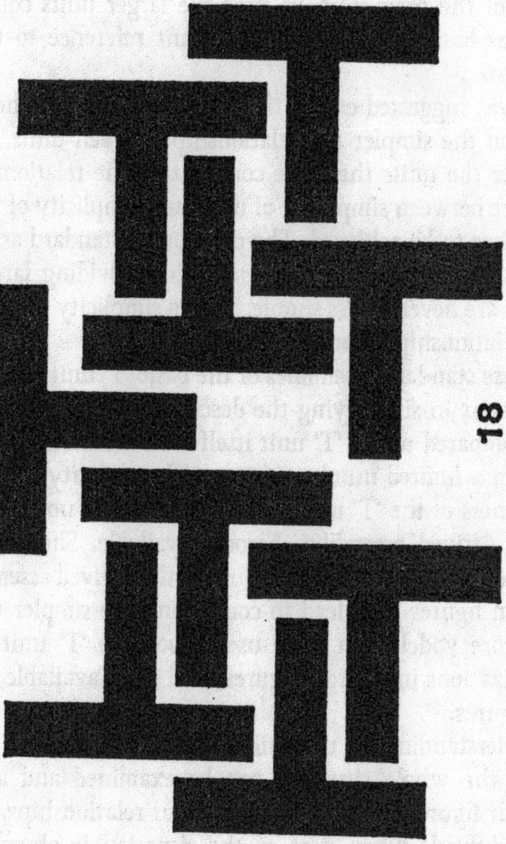

18

'T' units but into 'I' units, as shown in picture 20 (page 51). The relationship between the three 'I' units is straightforward. Each 'I' unit is, of course, two 'T' units placed stem to stem.

The larger the unit used, the simpler become the relationships. Standard assemblies of 'T' units come to be used instead of the basic unit. In time the larger units come to be used as basic units without constant reference to their 'T' content.

It was suggested earlier that the more complex the unit of division the simpler the relationship between units, and the simpler the units the more complicated the relationships. A balance between simplicity of units and simplicity of relationships has to be achieved. The creation of standard assemblies of basic units avoids the dilemma by providing large units which are nevertheless simple. Thus a simplicity both of units and relationships is achieved.

These standard assemblies of the basic 'T' unit have a great usefulness in simplifying the description of complex figures, but compared to the 'T' unit itself such assemblies are useful only in a limited number of cases. The mobility and general usefulness of the 'T' unit ensure its retention no matter how many derived assemblies become available. Should the 'T' unit be forgotten, then the failure of the derived assemblies to explain figures may lead to confusion. The simpler the unit the more widely can it be used. Both the 'T' unit and its organizations into larger figures need to be available as familiar figures.

Understanding an unfamiliar situation is difficult enough when the whole situation can be examined and available familiar figures can be tried in familiar relationships. It is far more difficult when part of the situation is obscured and cannot be examined. The part may be inaccessible because the instruments and methods of examination are inadequate. Instruments are but devices for converting into a form avail-

19

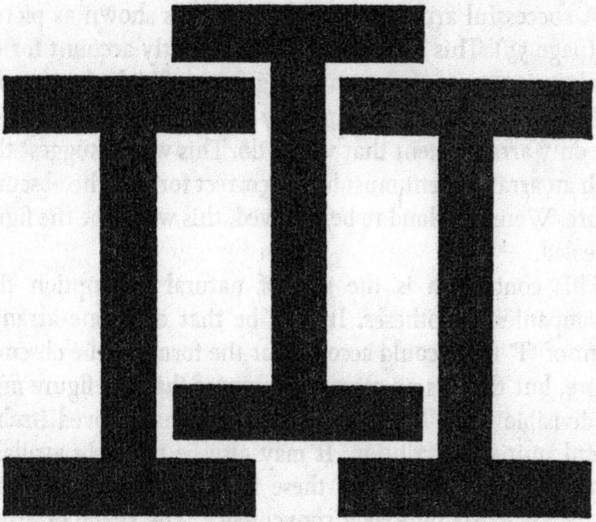

20

able to the senses a phenomenon which is not. Part of an unfamiliar situation may be inaccessible because the effort involved would be prohibitive. There may also be the simple physical impossibility of obtaining information from some part of the situation. Whatever the reason for such inaccessibility, an attempt is made to understand the whole situation by means of careful examination of as much of it as can be examined. A controlled guess or hypothesis is derived to explain the inaccessible portion.

Picture 21 (page 53) shows a figure of which part is obscured by an amorphous cloud. It is assumed that the figure is of a similar straight line format to those already encountered.

Careful examination and measurement of these pieces of the figure that emerge from the cloud can lead to various guesses as to what lies under the cloud. Different arrangements of the 'T' unit are tried in the hope that, if an arrangement describes the available part of the figure, it also describes the whole figure.

A successful arrangement of 'T' units is shown as picture 22 (page 55). This arrangement could exactly account for the unobscured parts of the preceding figure. Trial of every possible combination of 'T' forms may show that picture 22 offers the only arrangement that would do. This would suggest that such an arrangement must be the correct form of the obscured figure. Were the cloud to be removed, this would be the figure revealed.

This conclusion is the sort of natural assumption that accompanies hypotheses. It may be that only one arrangement of 'T' units could account for the forms of the obscured figure, but there is no reason to suppose that the figure must be divisible into 'T' units. The 'T' unit has proved itself a useful unit of description. It may also be the only available familiar figure. Neither of these facts changes its arbitrary nature. It exists only as a convenience. The shape of a new figure cannot be determined by a necessity to conform to

21

what is an arbitrary method of description. The strength of the 'T' unit built by its usefulness may easily suggest such a necessity. Another person with another familiar figure may decide that the obscured figure must be divisible into his own familiar figure.

It is true that the only possible hypothesis is in terms of available familiar figures (the 'T' unit in this case). Nevertheless, such an hypothesis, no matter how exact in 'T' terms, is only a guess and no proof that the figure must have this shape. The only proof of the hypothesis is its usefulness and so long as this persists the hypothesis can be retained. But even such usefulness should not preclude a search for a better hypothesis, perhaps using different familiar figures for explanation.

With the completely accessible figures encountered hitherto, one description is as good as another, but with partly obscured figures one hypothesis is as bad as any other.

Almost the entire business of thinking is taken up with trying to understand unfamiliar situations of either sort. Always there is some figure which must be arrived at by an arrangement of familiar figures. The arrangement of familiar figures is always directed towards some end. This is the practical way in which the ever-growing repertoire of familiar figures and relationships is used.

There is, however, another way in which the familiar figures can be used. They can be arranged in fanciful patterns, haphazardly or according to ideas of harmony. Such arrangements are purely for their own sakes.

Playing with the familiar figures in this way is not directed to any end, yet it can be very useful. The play process can turn up interesting patterns that become added to the repertoire of familiar figures and are just as useful as those acquired during description of unfamiliar figures. Such figures turned up by chance during play may provide the explanation to a hitherto unexplained figure. The very chance processes of

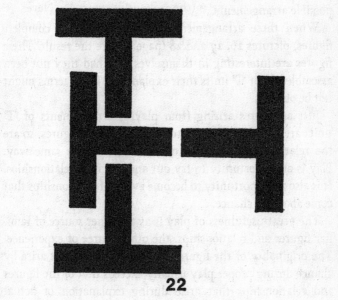

22

play provide combinations that may never have been thought of otherwise.

Pictures 23, 24 and 25 on page 57 show playful arrangements of the standard 'T' unit. There is no plan or intention behind the arrangements. Nor is there any reason for selecting these three arrangements out of the unlimited number of possible arrangements.

When these arrangements are assembled into complete figures, pictures 26, 27 and 28 (page 58) are the result. These figures are interesting in themselves, and had they not been assembled from 'T' units their explanation in 'T' terms might not be obvious.

Just as figures arising from playful arrangements of 'T' units are added to the repertoire of unfamiliar figures, so are the relationships which become familiar in the same way. Play is an opportunity to try out and test new relationships. It is also an opportunity to become aware of relationships that come about by chance.

The great usefulness of play is as the other source of familiar figures and relationships, the other source of experience. The originality of the figures and relationships that arise by chance during proper play usually exceeds that of the figures and relationships that arise during explanation of actual situations. Chance has no limits, but imagination has.

Even if the usefulness of play were accepted, very few people would find themselves able to play. It is difficult to do something deliberately which must not be deliberate. It is difficult to set off in a direction towards nowhere.

On page 59 is another figure of which the greater part is hidden by a black cloud of obscurity. This time even more of the figure is inaccessible to examination than on the previous occasion. It may be doubted whether anything useful at all can be deduced about the figure by examination of the visible parts. In the same way as before, various hypothetical ar-

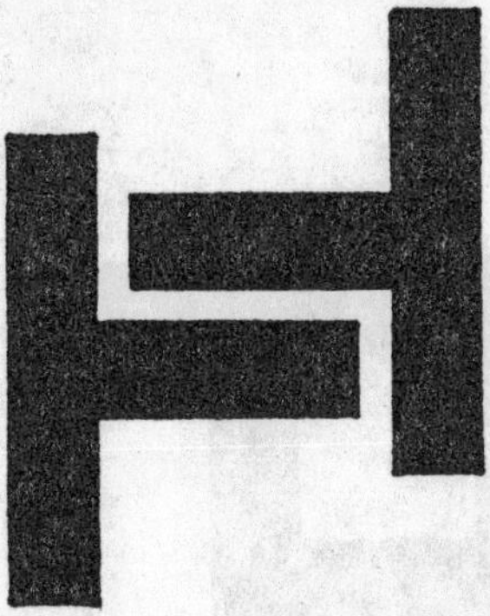

23

24

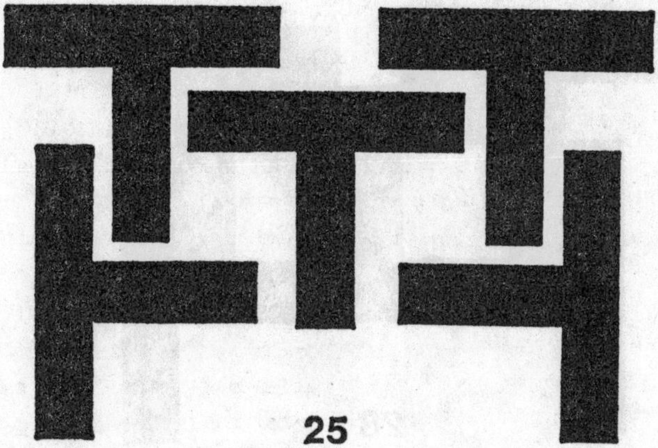

25

26

27

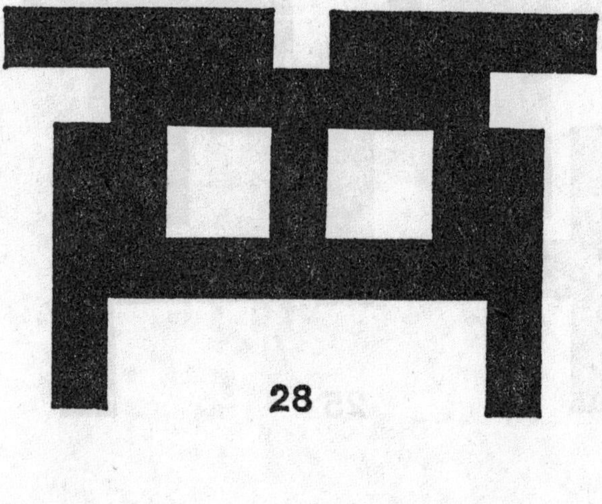

28

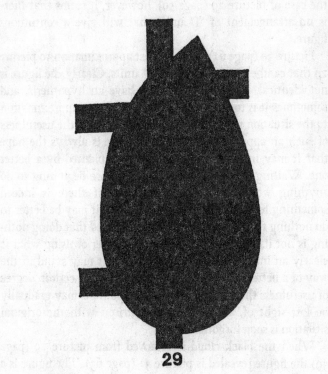

29

rangements of the basic 'T' unit can be tried. Whenever there are a number of hypothetical arrangements that all seem to fit the pattern, the impossibility of deciding which one to use makes it necessary to try to examine more of the figure. In the case of picture 29 (page 59), however, it seems that there is no arrangement of 'T' units that will give a continuous figure.

Picture 30 (page 62) is the nearest approximation to picture 29 that can be assembled out of 'T' units. Clearly the figure is not identical. If it is necessary to have an hypothesis, and sometimes it is for the sake of action, then an approximation to the situation may still be useful. Along with the usefulness of such an approximate hypothesis there is always the hope that it may improve with use or be supplanted by a better one. Waiting for a better hypothesis before beginning to do anything would seem less satisfactory if there is indeed something to be done. On the other hand, it may be better to do nothing than to make a mistake, provided that doing nothing is not itself a mistake. The main danger of using what is clearly an inadequate hypothesis is that it may stand in the way of a better one. With continued use and a certain degree of usefulness the inadequacy of the hypothesis may gradually be lost sight of, as the vivid comparison with the original situation is soon forgotten.

When the black cloud is removed from picture 29 (page 59) the figure revealed is picture 31 (page 63). The figure is a composition not of familiar 'T' units but of 'L' units. This may seem unfair since the only familiar figures allowed in this artificial game of experience have been the 'T' units. Far from being unfair, the introduction of the 'L' unit illustrates a very important point. The very cry of unfairness emphasizes this.

The point is that the 'L' unit is not something different from the 'T' unit. The 'L' unit is not a new, unfamiliar unit. Picture 32 on page 65 shows how the 'L' unit is derived from the 'T' unit by simply dropping off one of the arms. The 'L' unit has been implicit in the 'T' unit all along.

There is nothing sacred or immutable about the 'T' unit, even if its consistent usefulness may have suggested this. The 'T' unit will always be an arbitrary unit of convenience: a convenient unit into which unfamiliar figures can be resolved for the purpose of description. Just as a larger unit can be broken down into 'T' units, so can the 'T' unit itself be arbitrarily divided into smaller units.

It has already been seen how 'T' units can be arranged in standard assemblies to give the larger basic units which facilitate description of complex figures. It has been noted how these larger units, because of their size, have a less general usefulness than the 'T' unit. In the same way the 'T' unit can be considered a standard assembly of an 'L' and a short bar. Sometimes this standard assembly is too large and specific to describe a figure and must therefore be broken down into the smaller units with their wider application. So the 'T' unit may itself be broken down.

Building the 'T' unit up into larger units or breaking it down into smaller units are both possible, since the initial choice of the 'T' as the familiar unit was arbitrary. Had the 'L' unit been chosen initially, then the 'T' itself would have been derived from it. Any unfamiliar figure which was satisfactorily described by the 'T' unit would be described just as well by a combination of 'L' units and the short bars. The relationships involved in such descriptions would, however, be more complicated.

It is never easy to abandon familiar figures that have proved their usefulness over and over again. The sense of commitment is very strong. It is difficult to remember the arbitrary nature of the figure which seems to have been discovered, not just created to simplify descriptions. When an unfamiliar figure proves difficult to describe, great efforts are made to try every possible combination of well-tried familiar figures

30

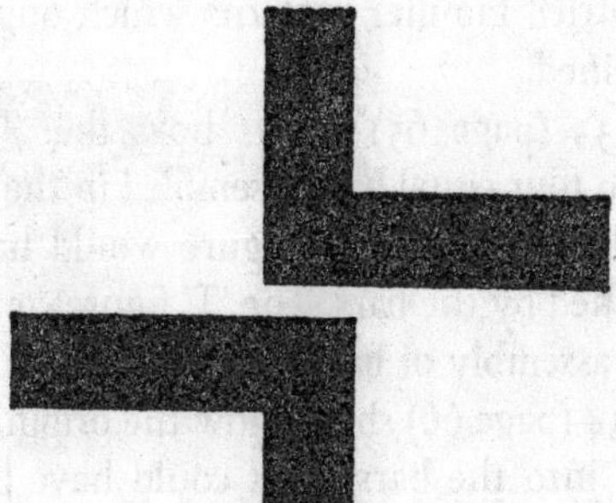

31

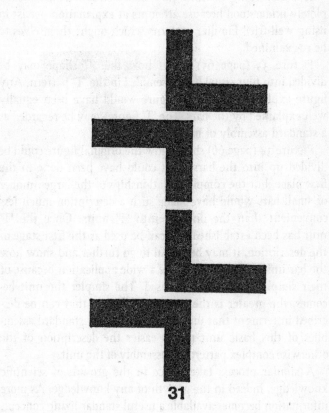

rather than some other figure. But there comes a time when it is necessary to question not the way familiar figures are put together in an explanation, but the familiar figures themselves.

It is disturbing to think how many situations are incompletely understood because attempts at explanation persist in using well-tried familiar patterns which ought themselves to be re-examined.

Picture 33 (page 65) shows how the 'T' shape may be divided into four equal bars assembled in the 'T' pattern. Any figure explained by the 'T' figure would have been equally well explained by the bars. The 'T' figures may be regarded as a standard assembly of bars.

Picture 34 (page 66) shows how the original figure could be divided up into the bars. This could have been done in the first place, but the complex relationships of the large number of small bars would have made such a description much less convenient than the division into 'T' units. Once the 'T' unit has been established and can be used as the first stage of the description, it may be useful to go further and show how the bar units, which must have a wide application because of their simplicity, can also be used. The simpler the unit becomes, the greater is the number of figures that can be described in terms of that unit. The provision of standard assemblies of this basic unit makes easier the description of the otherwise complex patterns of assembly of the unit.

A similar process takes place in the growth of scientific knowledge, indeed in the growth of any knowledge. As more information becomes available a useful standardizing concept, analogous to the 'T' unit, emerges and proves useful for explaining phenomena. As things seem to get more complicated, standard arrangements of the original concept prove useful. Finally there comes a situation which cannot be explained by the original concept or its standard assemblies. Suddenly an even simpler and more universal concept appears

32

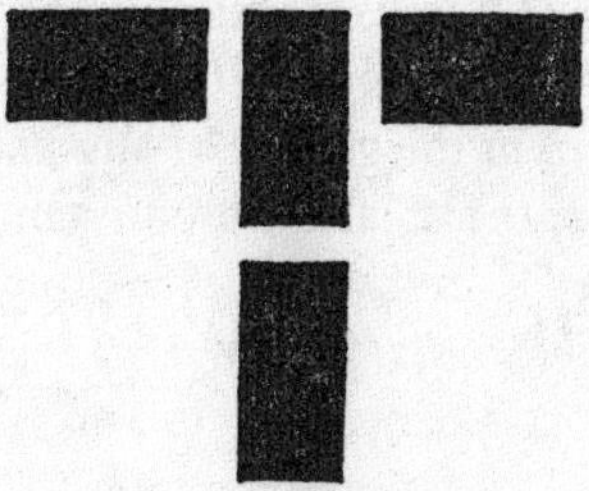

33

34

and the original concept is recognized as being a special derivative of this. This new concept, because of its simplicity, explains all the observed phenomena.

The original figure in this chapter would probably not have been described in the first place by means of the small bars because there would seem to be no point in such a complicated description. Also the relationships necessary to handle such a description might not yet have been available. It is in two easy stages that the description comes to use the bars. The first division into 'T' units is simple; then the division of the 'T' units themselves is also simple.

The difficulty is that there may seem to be no need to divide up the 'T' unit itself unless a certain situation shows it to be inadequate. Until such a situation is encountered, the 'T' unit may well be accepted as the simplest basic unit. There must be many situations which have been analysed only to the 'T' stage and which await a realization that further stages may be useful. Even the bar figure may not be the ultimate basic unit, if there can be such a thing. The bar can be divided into two squares, and so on.

Thus descriptions which started out using fairly large sub-figures and simple relationships end up by using very small and universal units also related in a simple manner. This simple manner is, however, obtained only by passing through stages which consist of standard assemblies of the basic units, then standard assemblies of the standard assemblies, and so on. The square becomes the bar, the bar the 'T' unit, the 'T' unit the 'I' unit.

At all stages the units of description are arbitrary, and though they may be very useful, complete commitment to them may prevent the emergence of a better description.

5

The principles of lateral thinking can be considered under four very general and certainly not exclusive headings. There is a good deal of fluidity, and some features could be considered under more than one heading or even given a separate heading. The headings are as follows:

1. Recognition of dominant polarizing ideas.
2. The search for different ways of looking at things.
3. A relaxation of the rigid control of vertical thinking.
4. The use of chance.

The recognition of dominant ideas has been mentioned in a previous chapter, and the present chapter deals with the search for different ways of looking at things.

The simple visual situations shown in the last chapter were intended to give a greater reality to the idea of lateral thinking than could be provided by mere words. It was seen that the original simple figure could be described in a variety of ways. Each of these ways was adequate in the sense that each gave a complete description. The choice of any particular way of describing the figure was arbitrary. The choice might have been made on the basis of convenience, simplicity or familiarity with the units used. At the time of choosing one particular way of looking at the figure, the observer would be aware of the arbitrariness of the choice, aware that another way could equally well have been chosen. But with time and as the convenience of the choice becomes more apparent the arbitrariness is forgotten and it is believed that the choice made is the only possible way of looking at the figure. With most situations, what starts as a temporary and provisional manner of looking at them soon turns into the only possible way, especially if encouraged by success. In time the figure which was once arbitrarily divided into 'T' units is seen to be no more than an arrangement of 'T' units.

The choice of a particular way of looking at things is usually casual and matter-of-fact. There is no intense scrutiny to find the best way. There is no question here of the malignant influence of a dominating idea, but only the simple necessity to look at something in some way. A bottle of wine is regarded as being half full by the optimist and half empty by the pessimist. One arbitrary way of looking at something seems just as good as another way. This may be so if one does not want to proceed any further than simple description, but if there is a problem to be worked out then the way it is looked at may make a very great deal of difference.

The pebble story showed a problem that seemed impossible to solve when looked at in one way, but surprisingly easy when the point of view was shifted. To solve the problem it was only necessary to look at the pebble that was left behind instead of at the one that was taken. The three-card trick is an exactly parallel example. The card-sharper offers three cards face down and invites the players to pick out the queen. By sleight of hand the player is at first allowed to win some money, and then in the same way the queen is made impossible to find. At this point the player could change his point of view and bet that the card he indicates is not the queen.

A very simple change in the way something is looked at can have profound effects. One of the most effective medical discoveries of all time came about when Edward Jenner shifted his attention from why people got smallpox to why dairymaids apparently did not. From the discovery that harmless cowpox gave protection against deadly smallpox came vaccination and the end of smallpox as a scourge in the western world.

In one of Sherlock Holmes's cases his assistant, Dr Watson, pointed out that a certain dog was of no importance to the case because it did not appear to have done anything. Sherlock Holmes took the opposite point of view and maintained that the fact that the dog had done nothing was of the utmost significance, for it should have been expected to do something, and on this basis he solved the case. It is said that the rulers of Europe in the early nineteenth century were much more concerned when the wily Austrian diplomat, Prince Metternich, appeared to do nothing than when he did something.

A shift from the obvious way of looking at something to a less obvious way may require no more than a shift of emphasis. This is not particularly difficult to do once one has got into the habit of trying to do it. With practice it becomes possible to find and try out several different ways of looking at a problem or situation. But first of all there must be an interest in trying to do so, an appreciation of the effectiveness of a change in point of view. The old and well-known problem of the two glasses, one filled with wine and the other filled with water, provides a neat illustration of the point. A spoonful of wine is taken from the wine-glass and stirred into the water-glass, then a spoonful is taken out of the water-glass and returned to the wine-glass. The operations are repeated. The problem is to tell whether there is more water in the wine-glass than there is wine in the water-glass or the other way round.

The problem is extremely tedious to work out if one goes through it stage by stage, assigning volumes to the spoon and glasses and finding the different concentrations of wine and water at each stage. If, however, the point of view is shifted so that the situation at the end is considered, instead of its development, the solution is very simple. Since each glass had

had two spoonfuls taken out and two returned, the volume at the end must be the same as at the beginning. Therefore any wine in the water-glass must have displaced an exactly equal volume of water, and this can only be in the wine-glass. The shift in attention may be from one part of the problem to another or from one stage in the development of the problem to another, but the basic way the problem as a whole is appreciated remains the same. It is relatively easy to shift attention in this way from one part of a problem to another, but much more difficult to change the parts themselves.

The mind divides the continuity of the world around us into discrete units. Partly this is made obligatory by the nervous organization of the brain and the consequent limited span of attention. Partly it is deliberately done in order to understand things by breaking them down into parts that are already familiar. This process was illustrated with the visual situations in the last chapter. It was seen that the parts were deliberately extracted from the whole situation and then fitted together by means of fixed relationships to re-create the whole. Thus a continuous process of change may be arbitrarily cut at some convenient point, and what goes before the cut may be linked to what goes after by the familiar relationship of cause and effect. The choice of the parts into which the whole is dissolved is dictated by familiarity, convenience and the availability of simple relationships with which to recombine them. A relationship is the record of how the two pieces fitted together before the division. When the same division has been made over and over again, the units come to acquire an identity of their own.

Like food packages on the shelves of a supermarket, the packets of information formed by established ways of dividing things up lie waiting for someone to select them and convert them into an interesting meal. Unfortunately the packets of information assembled in this manner tend to support the established point of view. To accept the pre-packaged information is to accept a commitment as to the way that information can be assembled into an idea.

The units of convenience, the packets of information, acquire a name. Once they acquire a name they are frozen and immutable, for a label is usable only if it has an unvarying meaning. It becomes necessary to regard the world as being built of named bricks which can be knocked out and examined in order to facilitate understanding of the whole. The notion of a concrete building that can be broken down into pieces of arbitrary size and shape is gone.

A walking-stick may be described as consisting of a curved end joined to the ferrule end by a straight middle section. It could also be described as being made up of two halves, one of which is curved. Another description would offer a long straight section topped by a short curved section. The imagination can divide up the stick into a great number of different parts, quite irrespective of the fact that the stick is really made out of a single piece of wood that has been curved at one end. This fluidity of description is maintained only so long as the parts are not given names. As soon as that happens, one description becomes appropriate and the rest just fanciful.

The availability of words and names fixes the way a particular situation can be looked at. The dynamic fluidity of lateral thinking – which is continually forming, dissolving and re-forming the parts of the situation in ever different shapes – is gone, and with it the chance to find the best way of looking at the situation. Once the parts have been horribly frozen by words, the best that can be done is to put the words together in different patterns; but this is often inadequate. In the last chapter it was seen that there came a time when no pattern of 'T' units could explain the situation. The situation could only be explained when the 'T' unit itself was altered.

The rigidity of words is associated with the rigidity of classifications. Again, the rigidity of classifications leads to rigidity in the way things are looked at. A recent film showed a final scene in which the hero and his friends celebrate on the deck of a warship as they watch an island blow itself to pieces. On the island were the bad lads, a team of wicked scientists who were using their power to try and control the world. The island was also crammed with apparently innocent people whom the scientists had brainwashed into submission. Since the scientists were classified as bad and the island as bad land, it seemed quite natural that (by classification) everyone on it should be blown to pieces.

New ideas tend to occur much more often to those who are able to escape from this rigidity of words and classifications. There is a story that during the war a pilot flying a bomber home began to have difficulty with the controls. A leakage in the hydraulic system was diagnosed, but there was no fluid available to top it up. In the end the crew were saved because someone thought of using urine to refill the system: a simple and apparently effective solution, but many people would never have thought of it because urine and hydraulic systems are named and classified so far apart. A similar example occurred in an unlit lane which was so narrow that cars which entered it had to reverse their way out again. Very few cars had reversing lights and there was always great difficulty in getting out without colliding with something. One day someone thought of using the traffic indicator which flashed brightly at the rear of the car and intermittently lit up the road. It worked very well. Presumably no one had thought of this simple solution before because the indicator was named and classified as an indicator and not a light.

One technique for avoiding the rigidity of words is to think in terms of visual images and not use words at all. It is perfectly possible to think coherently in this way and difficulty only arises when it is necessary to express what has been thought. Unfortunately not many people are good at thinking visually and not all situations can be examined in terms of visual images. Nevertheless it is a habit well worth acquiring, for visual images have a fluidity and plasticity that words can never achieve.

Visual thinking does not simply mean using the original visual pictures as the material of thought. That would be clumsy. The visual language of thought makes use of lines, diagrams, colours, graphs and many other devices to illustrate relationships that would be very cumbersome to describe in ordinary language. Such visual images alter shape easily under the influence of dynamic processes and it is also possible to show the past, present and future effects of a process all at the same time.

A very useful technique for escaping from the fixed parts of a problem is to break the parts down into still smaller parts and then recombine these smaller units to form larger novel units. This process was implicit in the way the 'T' unit in the previous chapter was altered. It is usually much easier to put together sub-parts in different formations than to divide the situation into novel parts from the first.

The number of different ways in which something can be looked at is limited not only by the rigidity of the available units of description but also by the number of available relationships. A small repertoire of known relationships inevitably means a marked sterility of view. The larger the repertoire of relationships that can be handled with confidence, the more original can be the lines of division, the ways of looking at a situation.

With some effort and much practice it becomes possible to find many more ways of looking at a situation than the most probable. Yet most of these other ways, perhaps all of them, will turn out to be of no value. Having made the effort to find them and taken the trouble to consider each of them in turn, one usually finds that they are not as useful as the obvious way of looking at the situation. Under what conditions is it worthwhile to use lateral thinking in this way, and under what conditions might one be content with vertical thinking?

The use of lateral thinking is essential in those problem situations where vertical thinking has been unable to provide an answer. The pebble story is an example of this sort of situation. The problem remained insoluble until unusual ways of looking at it were tried out. Other problems, like the wine and water problem, may be possible to solve by vertical thinking, but the process is tedious. In such cases lateral thinking, though not essential, may be of much help in providing a better solution. By definition a problem is a situation that demands an answer and by implication that answer is not obvious. Sometimes the situation is only a problem because it is looked at in a certain way. Looked at in another way, the right course of action may be so obvious that the problem no longer exists.

How often one turns to lateral thinking is a matter of temperament. If lateral thinking is used only when vertical thinking cannot solve a problem, then a certain amount of time is saved, but should there be lateral solutions to problems which can only just be solved by vertical thinking, these will always be missed. Someone who tries out lateral thinking on every problem will at first waste some time, but the practice that is acquired will make the process more and more rapid. Not only will the habit of mind so developed make lateral thinking far more effective when it really is needed but it may also produce dividends in the form of more effective answers to problems that do have a vertical solution.

In definite problem situations it is fairly easy to recognize the need for lateral thinking and new ideas, but in non-problem situations it is very much more difficult to see any need for it. It may be that the biggest problem is that there is no apparent problem. If everything seems to be proceeding smoothly and adequately, progress may be impossible because there is no problem which can be used as a step to improvement. Any enterprise that does not have problems does not have much chance of progress either. Problems are the jolts that shift things out of the smooth rut of mere adequacy. The most difficult problem often lies in the formulation of problems. It may require a good deal of lateral thinking to realize that there are problems which have not been recognized.

Towards the end of the last century physicists were very pleased with themselves. It seemed that everything that there was to explain had been explained. Theories and measurements fitted together neatly. All that remained to be done was to tidy things up. The role of physics would in the future consist in making ever more refined measurement within the broad outlines of the known theoretical structure. Then along came Planck and Einstein, and it soon became obvious that, far from being completed, physics had only just begun.

When are adequacy, complacency and absence of problems merely other names for inadequacy and lack of imagination? Is an apparently satisfactory way of looking at things satisfactory because every other way has been considered and found inferior, or because there has not seemed any need to consider other ways or enough imagination to find them?

The usual answer is to accept something as adequate until new information proves it to be inadequate. Why not reverse the process and develop a new way of looking at things, and then see if it proves useful? A reorganization of information does not have to await the impact of new facts; it can take place whenever anyone appreciates the arbitrary nature of a theory and proves competent to evolve a different one. Dissatisfaction with the old theory or simple curiosity may provide the motive.

It is not even possible to suppose that a theory which explains all available information is better than one which is incomplete. For practical purposes such a supposition is inescapable, but there have been instances where closed theories have been supplanted by theories which seemed inadequate at first, but turned out to have more potential. The physical explanation of an eclipse must have seemed very inadequate to believers in the manifestations of God's wrath until adequate data became available.

Too often it is assumed that no one has the right to doubt an explanation unless a better one is offered. This is a most effective way of inhibiting new ideas. How is it possible to put things together in a new way when the old way has to be kept intact until the new one is completed? To look for a new idea through the framework of the old is a waste of time. To compare the new way with the old way is useless and inhibiting.

The interpretation of a situation may be looked upon as an anagram. Things fit together and make sense, but this does not preclude their being put together in a new way which makes even more sense. Everyone has the right to doubt everything as often as he pleases, and the duty to do it at least once. No way of looking at things is too sacred to be reconsidered. No way of doing things is beyond improvement. It should be possible to look at a wheel and reconsider its efficiency.

It is a common fallacy to suppose that, whatever approach is chosen, a problem can always be solved if that particular approach is followed to its end with sufficient logical skill. There are vertical thinkers who resent any suggestion that logic is not omnipotent; they cannot see any use for lateral thinking. To them there is only one way of looking at a problem, and the other ways are only stages in the logical progression from this only way.

Ultimately there must be a stage of perceptual convenience which comes before logic. If this perceptual choice on which the whole structure of logic is built is incorrect, then the solution cannot be found. Lateral thinking avoids this limitation by trying one approach after another quite deliberately. Once the approach is chosen it is then pursued with the full vigour of vertical thinking. Then another approach is chosen, and so on. No amount of excellence on the part of an electronic computer can lead to the solution of a problem if the problem has been incorrectly defined by the programmer.

In tackling a problem it is common to assume a set of limits within which the solution must lie. The boundaries of the problem are defined by assumption and then within those boundaries vertical thinking proceeds to find a solution. Very often, however, the boundaries are imaginary and the solution may lie outside them. Take the apocryphal story of Columbus and the egg. When his friends taunted him, saying that discovering America was really easy since one only had to point west and keep going, he asked them to stand an egg on end. They tried but failed. Then Columbus took the egg, flattened one end and stood it up. Naturally his friends protested that they had thought the egg could not be damaged. His friends had assumed for the egg problem limits which did not in fact exist. But they had also assumed that it would not be possible to point west and keep on sailing. This feat of navigation seemed easy only after Columbus had shown that their assumptions were imaginary.

It seems more likely that the egg story really concerns the Italian architect Brunelleschi, who built the dome of the cathedral in Florence when everyone had assumed that such a dome could not be built. The historical accuracy of the story is of less importance than its customary assignment to Columbus in order to illustrate an attitude of mind.

Very often the lateral solution to a problem is regarded by vertical thinkers as a form of cheating. In a paradoxical way this proves the usefulness of lateral thinking. The stronger the accusations of cheating, the more obvious it is that the accusers have been bound by rigid rules and assumptions which do not in fact exist. In the same way the path to new ideas is blocked by false assumptions of one form or another. Vertical thinkers are very apt to make such assumptions because the effective use of logic requires a definite and rigidly defined context. Certain things must be accepted and taken for granted. The fluidity of a situation where nothing is rigid and everything is doubted all the time makes vertical thinkers extremely uncomfortable. Yet it is from this limitless potential of chaos that new ideas are formed by lateral thinking.

The search for alternative ways of looking at things is not natural. The natural tendency of the mind is to become impressed by the most probable interpretation, and then to proceed from that. In order to overcome this natural tendency it is necessary to be deliberate and even artificial. One technique that seems deceptively simple is to predetermine the number of ways in which any situation can be looked at. The number may be three, five or more. Each problem that is encountered is then deliberately looked at in this number of ways. At first the process seems very artificial. Many of the interpretations that are manufactured to order seem quite absurd when compared with the natural and obvious interpretation. Yet no matter how absurd the forced interpretations may seem, the quota must be filled. In time and with practice it becomes less of an effort to find other ways of looking at a situation, and these other ways seem very nearly as reasonable as the most obvious way.

Another useful technique is to turn upside down deliberately by consciously reversing some relationship. Instead of looking at the walls of a house as support for the roof, the walls may be considered as suspended from the roof. Instead of moving an aeroplane through the air so that the wings may build up lift, keep the body of the plane still and only move the wings through the air, as in a helicopter. Instead of assuming that the sun moves round the earth, assume that the earth moves round the sun. Instead of something moving in a curve through space, assume that space itself is curved. To reverse or otherwise alter a relationship as in these instances is easy, because wherever a direction is defined the opposite direction is, by implication, equally defined.

A further technique for breaking down the rigidity of a particular way of looking at things is to transfer the relationships of the situation to another more easily handled situation. Thus an abstract situation may be turned into a concrete analogy. The value of this procedure is twofold. In the first place the restrictions on ways of looking at the original situation are not carried over to the analogy, which can be altered much more easily. If a fertile analogy is chosen, then the relationships may easily be played around with. Periodically the original situation is looked at again in the light of alterations in the analogy, and this process stimulates new ideas, new approaches. The second advantage is that analogies usually make use of concrete images, which suggest other concrete images much more readily than abstract ideas suggest other abstract ideas, and as a result the flow of ideas proceeds more easily.

Another simple technique is deliberately to shift emphasis from one part of a problem to another. For this purpose it does not matter if the problem is defined in the most obvious way so long as each part of it is placed in turn under the spotlight of attention. Even the most insignificant part of the problem ought to be deliberately given its fair share, and this is much more difficult than it sounds. The pebble story has a happy ending only when attention is shifted from the pebble that is taken to the one that is left.

Perhaps the clearest example of the benefit to be derived from looking at things in different ways is to be found in mathematics. Any equation whatsoever is no more than the putting down of two different ways of describing something. Yet the usefulness of having two ways instead of one is so great that it is one of the corner-stones of mathematics. Having the two different ways of looking at something on either side of the equals sign makes it possible to manipulate the whole thing into an answer. With lateral thinking a rapid succession of different ways of looking at something are deliberately passed through the mind. The time and probability properties of the brain then automatically effect the interaction of these different approaches to yield an effective answer.

6

The third basic principle of lateral thinking is the realization that vertical thinking by its nature is not only ineffective in generating new ideas but also positively inhibiting. There is an extreme type of temperament which compulsively seeks for tight control of what goes on in the mind: everything has to be logically analysed and synthesized. There is a striving for a meticulousness and precision which is as artificial as a strip of cine-film which divides motion up into a series of static images. This is an extreme type of mind, but there are a great number of minds which show this inclination to lesser degrees.

In the last chapter it was suggested that vertical thinking needed as a starting point a basic accepted structure which could then be extended or modified as it was worked upon. Although this can lead to alterations in the accepted idea it is unlikely to lead to a completely new idea. Acceptance and commitment are the very opposite of the limitless potential of chaos.

Stone by stone, a causeway is constructed by logic through the mud of unformed ideas. Each stone is firm and correctly placed. Indeed, each successive stone can be placed only if one is standing firmly on the one previously laid. With logical control it is necessary to be right at every stage – that is the very essence of logic.

But with lateral thinking it is not necessary to be right all the time. It is only the final conclusion that must be correct. Lateral thinking means getting down into the mud and searching around until a natural causeway is found. The need to be right at every stage and all the time is probably the biggest bar there is to new ideas.

As Marconi increased the power and efficiency of his equipment he found that he could send wireless waves over longer distances. Finally he became bold enough to think about transmitting a signal across the Atlantic Ocean itself. It seemed only a matter of having a powerful enough transmitter, a sensitive enough receiver. The experts who knew better laughed at the idea. They assured him that since wireless waves, like light, travelled in straight lines, they would not follow the curvature of the earth, but would stream off into space. Logically the experts were quite right. But Marconi tried, persisted and succeeded in sending a signal across the Atlantic. Neither Marconi nor the experts knew about the electrically charged layer in the upper atmosphere, the ionosphere, which bounced back the wireless waves that would otherwise have streamed off into space as predicted by the experts. It was only this layer which made communication possible. By being wrong Marconi arrived at a conclusion he could never have reached had he been rigidly logical all along.

The discovery of adrenalin came about through a mistaken impression. A certain Dr Oliver had developed a gadget which he thought measured the diameter of that artery at the wrist which is used for feeling the pulse. He measured the diameter of this artery in his son under a variety of conditions. One of the conditions involved the injection of an extract of calves' adrenal glands. He thought he detected that this injection decreased the size of the artery. We now know that the effect of adrenalin on the diameter of a large artery would be undetectable. Dr Oliver rushed off to let the world know of his discovery. The world, as represented by Professor Schafer, a renowned physiologist, was disbelieving. But Dr Oliver's enthusiasm eventually persuaded the professor to inject some of the extract into a dog whose blood pressure was being measured. To his amazement the blood pressure rose in an extraordinary fashion. Adrenalin had been discovered.

It is possible to point out many other instances where an effective discovery came at the end of a line of reasoning which was certainly not correct at every stage. It is like walking over a rocky beach. One way is to move slowly and cautiously; making sure that at each step you are firmly balanced on the rock on which you are standing before you take another step. The other way is to move swiftly over the rocks pausing so briefly on each that a precise balance at every step is no longer required. When you have got somewhere interesting, that is the time to look back and pick out the surest way of getting there again. Sometimes it is very much easier to see the surest route to a place only after you have arrived. You may have to be at the top of a mountain to find the easiest way up.

The purpose of logic should be not so much to find the final conclusion but to make sure that it is sound once it has been found. There is no doubt that this proof should be as precise and rigorous as possible. But this sort of proof can just as easily be applied to a conclusion that has been reached by lateral thinking as to one that has been reached by vertical thinking.

It may be argued that there can be no harm in using vertical thinking to reach the final conclusion even though this conclusion could be reached by lateral thinking. Unfortunately there may be positive disadvantages in using vertical thinking for this purpose, and the apparent economy of effort is an illusion, for valid vertical thinking must exclude alternatives at every step, whereas lateral thinking is not forced to make this effort. The first positive disadvantage is that if vertical thinking is successful in finding a route to the final conclusion, then there will seem to be no need to look for a better and more direct route. With lateral thinking, however, a sound route must be sought after the point is reached, and since there is no commitment to a partially adequate route a better one may be found.

The second disadvantage concerns the direction taken by the logical route. We use logic in looking for new ideas because that is the only way we know how to move. There must be a direction in which to move, a direction in which to exert effort. So the direction best signposted from where we are standing at the moment is the one chosen. This is the high road of vertical thinking, and along it we can move vigorously. But moving vigorously in the wrong direction may be worse than not moving at all. This is not an argument for doing nothing, but a suggestion that instead of striking off vigorously in the most obvious direction, one ought perhaps to spend the same amount of energy spiralling round the problem.

The high road of vertical thinking leads straight towards what seems to be the solution to the problem, but the most effective solution may require that one proceed in exactly the opposite direction. It is a simple experiment to separate an animal from food by a wire screen through which it can see the food. With certain species (e.g. domestic fowl) the animal will look straight at the food and try hard to get through the screen. At a higher level of intelligence (e.g. a dog), the animal realizes that to get the food it must first of all go away from the food and get round the wire screen. It is easy enough to make this detour when an obstacle obstructs the most obvious route towards a solution, but it is not so easy to choose to go in the opposite direction when there is no apparent obstacle. When the two women, each claiming to be the mother of an infant, were brought before King Solomon, he ordered the baby to be cut in half and half given to each woman. Since his chief concern was presumably to see that justice was done and to save the baby, this order went in directly the opposite direction. Yet the ultimate effect was to discover the real mother, who preferred to let the other woman have the baby rather than see it killed.

As lateral thinking does not have any fixed direction there is no difficulty in going away from a problem in order to solve it. If you are stopped on a hill and the car in front of you starts to slip back towards you, the natural thing is to try to reverse away (assuming there is a stream of traffic in the other lane). It may, however, make more sense to do the opposite and to drive up to the car in front. This lessens the impact, and at this point the additional brakes of your car may be sufficient to hold the one that is slipping back.

If the necessity to be right at every stage is one limitation of vertical thinking, another one is the necessity to have everything rigidly defined. The compulsively logical mind likes everything to be cut and dried. Such a mind is uneasy with variation : a word must always mean the same thing and cannot change its meaning temporarily in order to accommodate a flow of ideas. A lateral thinker may step fleetingly on a word, using it only as a brief foothold in his passage : the vertical thinker must balance squarely on it, acknowledging its firm rigidity.

The vertical thinker is for ever classifying things, because in this way vagueness can be controlled. The vertical thinker is more interested in seeing on what basis he can pull things apart, the lateral thinker is more interested in seeing on what basis he can put things together.

Some minds even carry this passion for rigid classification to the lengths of trying to capture ideas with a symbol and then relating them to other ideas with further symbols. This sort of mathematical definition may make it easier to handle ideas, but it also restricts them to a definiteness they may not naturally offer. The confining rigidity of a symbol is a form of commitment that effectively prevents the free contraction and expansion of an idea that may be necessary for its development. The water in the well is not defined by the shape of the receptacles that are used for withdrawing it. There is no doubt that western efficiency and progress are based on the mathematical method, but not everything that goes on in the mind can be handled in this way all the time. It is far more fruitful to alternate between periods of creative fluidity and periods of developmental rigidity.

Much of the difficulty with classifying is that the mind prefers static definitions. We talk of 'grey' as a definite classification, not just a stage in the dynamic process of black becoming white. The difference between a static and a dynamic definition is that the latter is not really a definition at all, but merely a possibility. The fluidity of possibility does not inhibit the emergence of new ideas as does the rigidity of being.

Some time ago I became interested in finding out whether the mind could experience a visual hallucination which it knew to be a logical contradiction. With hypnosis it is quite easy, while a subject is in a trance, to suggest that on a given signal the subject will experience a particular hallucination. The subject is then woken up and some time later the signal word is given. The effect can be striking. If the hallucination is that of a person entering the room the subject may get up, shake hands with the person who is not there, introduce him all round and talk to him. The subject also gets very upset that no one else is taking any notice of the person. Using the same method I tried to get a subject to hallucinate a square circle after he had come out of the trance: he was to see the square circle as a figure drawn on the wall. When the signal word was given the effect was extraordinary. The subject declared emphatically that he could see the figure which was at once a perfect square and a perfect circle. At the same time he acknowledged that this was not logically possible. So real was the impression that he grabbed a pencil and tried to copy what he could see. No sooner had he begun to draw than he would scratch it out and try again, as with frantic frustration he sought to draw what could not be drawn. This was not intended as an exercise in synthetic mysticism, but an inquiry into whether the mind could hold vividly in consciousness an experience which it acknowledged to be impossible on logical grounds. In its early stages an idea might exist in a form too contradictory for logical acceptance. This does not mean that it cannot develop into a useful new idea.

The first intimations of a new idea may be too nebulous to be captured and arranged for logical presentation. There is a natural inclination to pounce on such an idea and drag it out into full consciousness by giving it a definite form and shape. Before the idea has had a chance to grow in a haphazard (and original) fashion, it is organized and given shape. But the shape is one that has been chosen for the idea, not the one it might have grown into on its own. The free flight of the idea is curtailed, and it is as firmly fixed as a butterfly to the collector's board. Pouncing on an idea as soon as it appears kills the idea. Too early and too enthusiastic logical attention either freezes the idea or forces it into the old moulds. Concentration on an idea isolates it from its surroundings and arrests its growth. The glare of attention inhibits the fertile semi-conscious processes that go to develop an idea.

It is quite true that without early logical attention the mind is capable of entertaining in vague form such fancy notions as perpetual motion machines. It is quite true that on occasions, for instance under the effect of LSD, the mind is convinced that it has found the secret of the universe. It is quite true that only rapid logical attention can flush the mind of such time-wasting fantasies. But it may be better to run the risk of harbouring occasional perpetual motion fantasies than to risk scouring out all manner of useful ideas through the vigorous use of logic at too early a stage. It is better to have enough ideas for some of them to be wrong than to be always right by having no ideas at all.

Expressing an idea is an excellent way to organize it and

organization usually means logical arrangement. Too early expression may commit an idea to a pattern of development it may not naturally have followed.

Often the too early use of vertical thinking is due to a lack of confidence in lateral thinking. Without some confidence that a new idea will mature on its own, there must always seem a duty to do something about it. A new idea does not need to be moulded, it can be watched and followed as it grows and temporarily neglected when it does not. If an idea does not form itself into a usable shape there is not much to be gained from forcing it into one.

A mind which has too few new ideas can be excused an eagerness to rush at them: but in general an idea is far more fertile if seduced rather than raped. When an idea has matured and is ready for close examination, then it will be embarrassingly forward in its insistence: there will not be any possibility of hiding from it. When an idea is not ready, logical strictness will not mature it faster.

The finest way to treat an idea is to try it out: yet a practical illustration of the dangers of too early attention to an idea may be seen where the facilities to try out ideas can be easily obtained. As soon as an idea tentatively appears, it is quickly worked into a form suitable for an experimental project. The experiment is designed and the equipment obtained. At once the idea is frozen at what may have been an intermediate stage in its development. It is true that the idea may mature even as it is being tried out, but this is less likely, and furthermore there are not many minds that will allow it to do so and risk rendering obsolete the current apparatus and experiments. If the equipment cannot be obtained so readily an idea can sometimes mature to a point where a different sort of equipment may be necessary. In my own experience I have often ordered equipment which has been rendered obsolete before it was ever used by further development of an idea. This is not an argument against the ready availability of equipment, but an illustration of the dangers of too early organization of an idea.

Since it would be impractical to try out every single new idea, there has to be some form of selection. Logical judgement is the economic valve that intervenes between the conception of an idea and trial of its effectiveness. Only those ideas which pass this test get as far as a practical trial. The test is an attempt to bring about entirely within the mind the meeting between the idea and the real world in which it will have to work. As a first stage the logical judgement is carried out by the originator of the idea, but even if enthusiasm carries the idea through there are few ideas that can be actually tried out without the approval of someone else who controls the means of trying them out.

The above system would work very well were it not for the necessity of the logical judgement to be based on past experience. Logical judgement can take into account only those factors of which it is aware: it can deal only with such facts as are available. The mental model of the world in which the new idea is tried out is necessarily incomplete, based as it is on the incompleteness of experience.

When the cyclotron, that essential tool in the development of atomic energy, was first proposed, many experts were sure that it could not work. Fortunately they did not control implementation of the idea, for their judgement, based on the available evidence, was probably sound. Yet the idea worked, for an unforeseen effect of the magnetic field on completion prevented the lack of efficiency which had been predicted. In this case and in that of Marconi, logical judgement was right according to the known facts and it was these which were insufficient.

Logical judgement can also be just plain wrong. When Dr Robert Goddard developed his idea for rocket propulsion and proposed that this was the only feasible form of power for space travel, many people maintained that a rocket could not work in space because there would be nothing for the rocket to push against. This was a misconception of the behaviour of rockets, which are propelled forward because the momentum of the hot gases rushing backward must be matched by the momentum of the rocket cases, which therefore have to move forward.

Many were the calculations which proved that heavier-than-air machines could not possibly fly. In the very same year that the Wright brothers first flew, the American Congress passed a special bill forbidding the army to waste any more money on trying out flying machines, for Langley of the Smithsonian Institute had used army money to build an unsuccessful plane. (Ironically, his plane, which crashed on take-off, was subsequently shown to be capable of flight.) At that same time patent offices were refusing applications for flying machines much as they refuse applications for perpetual motion machines today.

Descartes, one of the world's greatest thinkers, proved quite logically that the vacuum effects which Torricelli claimed were not possible. Torricelli, however, was able to support almost a metre of mercury with his vacuum, in spite of Descartes' views. He also arranged a trial in which four horses could not pull apart two plates which enclosed a vacuum.

For a long time the tangential fans which now form the basis of most of the neat domestic fan-heaters were assumed to be impossible. Someone had shown on physical principles that they could not work. It was many years before someone else came along and found out that they could work after all.

Nevertheless, no matter how incorrect logical judgement may often be, on occasions it remains essential as a mode of selection, since it would be impractical to carry out every idea. One can, however, temper its use with an awareness of its fallibility and even go against its decree when an idea can be tried out with but little effort.

It is sometimes a useful technique to try to be deliberately wrong in the evaluation of an idea. Instead of rapidly rejecting an idea which seems logically absurd, one accepts it and from it proceeds as far as one can in each direction – that is, downwards, to find its supports, and upwards, to see what it would lead to. This is much more difficult than it seems, and requires a good deal of practice. The purpose of such perversity is to question the accepted point of view on which was built the original logical rejection. In defending an apparently incorrect idea, a better point of view can often be discovered.

Not only can the existing logical context lead to summary dismissal of an idea but it may lead to the ignoring of a very good new idea which does not fit into the context. There is nothing more sad than a new idea which is at first ignored and then much later discovered. Apparently the electrically charged layer in the atmosphere which enabled Marconi to send the first wireless waves across the Atlantic had been suggested by Balfour Stewart many years before, but the idea had been too new to be noticed. It was not until Marconi's success had provided a suitable context that the idea was again taken up and the existence of the ionosphere finally proved by Breit and Tuve in 1925.

When Gregor Mendel humbly yet proudly presented the results of his experiments with plants to the Brün Society for the study of natural diseases, there was no interest at all in the matter. The genius of this simple monk and the fact that the tremendously important science of genetics had been born meant nothing to an audience who were listening to yet another careful gardener with his pet theories. It was many years before the report was re-discovered and given its full importance.

With lateral thinking one wanders and wonders. Something may be noticed for the pure sake of noticing. There is no attempt to explain it at once, no attempt to give it an importance. The thing is just noticed. If it gives rise to an idea, then so much the better: if not, there is no attempt to wring an idea from it. Later on it might prove useful. But it is noted in its pure form, unaltered by consideration of importance or having to fit into a context. In this way the richness of an open consciousness embraces all that is offered without the need to explain or classify or construct at every instant. It is in such a context that chance works to generate new ideas. But that is the subject of the next chapter.

7

The fourth basic principle of lateral thinking is the use of chance in the generation of new ideas. It may seem paradoxical to suggest that something can be done about chance, for by definition chance events cannot be brought about by design. That is precisely their value in leading to new ideas. Yet chance processes can still be used profitably. The solid wealth of insurance companies and the success of those who organize gambling are some indication of the profits to be derived from the efficient use of chance.

Without interfering with the chance processes themselves it is possible to use them deliberately by providing a suitable setting in which they may take place, and then harvesting the results of the chance interactions. Imagine that you were playing a game of chance such as roulette, with someone else's money. You were permitted to keep your winnings but your losses were paid for you. The result would be a sort of one-way roulette at which you could not lose. At any particular moment you could not be sure of winning on the next play, but you would know that if you played long enough you would win. You would hardly refuse to play because the process is not predictable and not entirely within your control. On the contrary, you would play as often as you could in order to increase your chances of winning. Using this model it is possible to see what can be done about chance processes in thinking. The first step is to be aware that there is the possibility of playing this game of one-way roulette, and this also means being aware of the sort of prizes that can be won. The second step is to learn how to play. The third step is to play as often as you can and to get rid of any inhibitions which interfere with your playing. The fourth step is to learn to recognize when you have won and to pick up your winnings instantly. This fourth step is worth considering a little further. With roulette there might be no difficulty in picking up your winnings, but suppose the game was so complicated that you could not at first always realize that you had some winnings (and if you did not pick them up they would be lost). The chance processes themselves would not change, but as you got better and better at recognizing when you had won, your winnings would increase.

The first step is to acknowledge the valuable contributions to progress that have been initiated by chance events, that is, events which did not occur by design. Wireless waves were discovered when Hertz noticed a tiny spark playing on a piece of apparatus across the room from the equipment he was using. X-rays were discovered when Roentgen forgot to remove a specially prepared fluorescent screen from a table on which he was playing with a cathode ray tube. The use of silver salts to make paper light-sensitive for photography was discovered when Daguerre and his associate noticed the image left by a silver spoon which had been lying on an iodized metal surface. These are but a selection of the many ideas that were started off by a chance arrangement of factors. In many cases it is difficult to see how else the ideas could have come about. There are far too many chemicals for it to have been possible for Daguerre to have searched through them all in order to find a suitable light-sensitive one. Roentgen and Hertz would not even have searched for X-rays and wireless waves because they were unaware that there was anything to search for.

Most people can remember in their own experience a number of significant events which happened by chance. Not long ago I was looking for a certain article in a scientific journal. I had a note of the name of the journal, the year, the volume and the page number. Taking the appropriate volume from the library shelf, I opened it at the right page number and found an article of great significance for the work I was doing at that moment. This article was far more useful than the one I had been looking for – but it was quite a different article. What had happened was that the journal had a supplement which looked exactly the same and on the very same page number of the supplement (which I had taken instead of the journal proper) began the unlooked-for article.

It is not only single chance events that can lead to new ideas. Sometimes a whole chain of circumstances provide the background. As a young man Alexander Fleming could not afford a medical education. While he was in London doing something else he happened to play in a game of water-polo against a team from St Mary's Hospital. When a relative died and unexpectedly left a legacy just large enough for Fleming to enter medical school, he chose St Mary's Hospital because he had had this brief contact with it. It so happened that at St Mary's worked Sir Almroth Wright, the great bacteriologist, who was interested in the way the body dealt with bacterial infection and was developing the theory and practice of inoculation. Soon Fleming became interested in these matters and found himself in the best possible environment and with the best possible teacher in this field. During the First World War Fleming had to deal with battle casualties and he became increasingly dissatisfied with the current disinfectants, which damaged the tissue as much as they damaged the bacteria. Many years later Fleming was culturing a drop of nasal discharge and noticed that it seemed to inhibit bacterial growth. From this observation he discovered lysozyme, a natural antibiotic which was harmful to bacteria but harmless to man. Unfortunately its effects were very weak.

It was against this background that Fleming one day noticed that a culture plate had become contaminated by a mould from the atmosphere. This is a common and annoying happening but Fleming, instead of throwing the plate away, noticed how the bacterial growth had been stopped around the mould. The extraordinary chance at this point is that the *Penicillium notatum* mould was only one of several hundred moulds which might have settled on the plate. Not one of the others has anything like the same effect. In fact even the colossal resources and efforts of modern science specifically looking for a mould have not been able to find anything quite as competent as this mould which arrived by chance.

The chain of events does not even end there. Fleming noted the behaviour of penicillin on human infections, but lacked the chemical competence to make it stable enough for regular use. Many years elapsed before Chain and others at Oxford decided quite arbitrarily to investigate the chemical problems involved. Then things moved rapidly, and the impetus of the Second World War made penicillin into a practical and amazingly effective antibiotic.

The water-polo match that determined the choice of St Mary's Hospital and led to Sir Almroth Wright, the unexpected legacy, the war experience, the discovery of lysozyme, the plate contaminated by chance with the most powerful of moulds, the decision to investigate the chemical stabilization of penicillin – these form a chain of events that were not put together by any logical construction.

With hindsight it is always possible to construct significant chains of events that led up to great ideas. By themselves they prove nothing. But they do show that chance is useful in providing something to look at when that something could never have been looked for.

If the purpose of chance in generating new ideas is to provide one with something to look at which one would not have looked for, then there may be methods of encouraging this process. Play is probably the ideal method. It must, however, be true purposeless play without design and direction. Just as a carefully designed experiment is an attempt to hurry nature along the path of logical investigation, so play is an attempt to encourage the chance appearance of phenomena which would not be sought out. Playing around is an experiment with chance. It is by no means easy to play in this fashion, for deliberate and earnest efforts at play defeat its purpose.

The very uselessness of play is its greatest asset. It is this freedom from design or commitment that allows chance to juxtapose things which would not otherwise have been arranged in this way, to construct a sequence of events which would not otherwise have been constructed. The apparent uselessness of play naturally discourages people from playing. Vertical thinkers are ashamed to play, but the only shameful thing is the inability to play.

James Clerk Maxwell, one of the very greatest scientific and mathematical geniuses, was for ever playing. In the midst of a dinner party he would be lost to the other diners as he fiddled with the cutlery, a reflection from a glass, or a drop of water. Clerk Maxwell knew the value of play, for as a teenager he had started his scientific career by playing around with pins and threads after he had been taken to a lecture given by Hay, an artist who obtained his effects in this way. With pins and thread Clerk Maxwell learned how to draw ellipses, and from this he went on to explain the laws of reflection of light when he was still so young that someone else had to read his paper to the Edinburgh Royal Society, since no one in short trousers was allowed to.

Why do children stop playing? It could be because the world changes from an unknown place in which wonderful things can happen into a familiar place in which there is an adequate explanation for everything. It could be this boredom of superficial familiarity that stops children playing. But if one is not content with glib explanations, then things can never be familiar enough to make play boring. It could be that play is actively discouraged by logical adults who point out its uselessness and define growing up as the responsibility to behave usefully.

During play ideas suggest themselves and then breed further ideas. The ideas do not follow one another in a logical progression, but if the mind makes no attempt to direct the ideas and is curious enough to pursue them, there will always be enough ideas – often there will be too many. The ideas may not prove useful immediately, but have a habit of turning up later. Even if no specific idea turns up, the general familiarity with a situation which is provided by playing around can prove a most useful background for the development of future ideas.

Another method of encouraging the chance interaction of ideas is the old one of brainstorming. A group of people gathered together to discuss a problem try to lay aside their usual logical inhibitions and say whatever comes into their minds: no thought is too absurd or irrelevant to be uttered. It takes a good deal of practice for a person to be able to offer less than logical thoughts and to refrain from censoring such thoughts when offered by others. The hope is that the mutual stimulation will give rise to many ideas and that chance interactions of these will produce new ideas that none of the participants would otherwise have thought of.

A useful technique for exciting new ideas is to expose oneself deliberately to a multitude of stimulants by wandering around a place that is full of things which would not be deliberately sought out. A general store, or an exhibition, or even a library could provide such a setting and it is more useful if the setting is not directly appropriate. Nothing is deliberately looked for, but instead of a searching attitude there is a readiness to consider anything that attracts the attention. Often it is the most irrelevant objects that are capable of stimulating the mind towards a new idea. Nor is there any need to analyse or assign an importance to whatever is noticed. It is a junk-collecting attitude: anything that catches the attention for whatever reason is picked out. All the time in the back of the mind is the problem for which the new idea is required.

In the course of wandering around something that looks as if it ought to be useful may be acquired though no definite use can be seen for it. The object is then left lying around and gradually it becomes associated with all the different aspects of the original problem. In a passive way it exerts an influence – perhaps an organizing influence. One day the casually acquired object is found to play a significant part in the emergence of a new idea. This technique does not apply to physical objects but could be used with other ideas or theories that are casually acquired.

A further method of encouraging the chance interaction of ideas involves the deliberate intertwining of the many separate lines of thought that may at different times occupy the mind. Instead of keeping the lines of thought rigidly separate in the usual manner, instead of concentrating on one subject with the deliberate exclusion of other distracting matters, everything is allowed to proceed concurrently with changes from one line to another being accepted as often as they occur. Thoughts developed in the pursuit of one subject are borrowed to advance another. Ways of looking at things which are conventional in one field become original when they intrude into another.

Scientists are fond of using the excuse of serendipity to obtain support for work which does not seem to have an immediate practical application. The idea is that in the course of their search for something they may stumble across something quite different and of great value. In general experiments are designed as a forcing house for information. An experiment is an attempt to organize nature into producing straight away information which would either not be available at all or else take too long to appear on its own. In an attempt to prove or disprove some theory the experimenter carefully organizes happenings to the best of his knowledge, ingenuity and technical ability; but experiments do not always work out as intended. Many a scientist who has set out to do one experiment has ended up doing another. Even if an experiment goes completely wrong the reason why it has not worked may actually yield more information than if it had worked. Sometimes an experiment may be working perfectly well, but an incidental observation at some point leads to an important discovery and the original experiment is never completed.

The difference between the emergence of a new idea through chance interactions and the careful construction of a theory by logical means may be illustrated by an analogy with paper-clips. A chain may be made out of paper-clips by carefully and deliberately attaching one clip to another. A chain can also be formed in quite a different way by opening out the clips a bit and then tossing them together in a pan. If they are tossed long enough and vigorously enough a chain-like structure may be lifted out at the end. A chain has been formed by the chance interaction and intertwining of the clips. With this second method the clips form themselves into a pattern which is always unexpected and usually original. Once the pattern is formed it can, of course, be trimmed and modified. If a strong chain of clips is required, then it may be better to use the method of deliberate arrangement. With the deliberate method, however, the chain is formed according to a definite plan and the final form of the chain cannot be any different from the plan. The deliberate chain may be likened to the high-probability way of arranging information and the tossing method may be likened to a low-probability method that makes use of chance.

The efficiency of the tossing method is much reduced if there are but few clips in the pan and also if the clips are not opened out but arranged in tight complete little chains. Likewise chance interactions are unlikely to generate new ideas if the information input is strictly limited to relevant information and if the available information is tied into tight little bundles already. For chance processes to be effective the information imprisoned in old and rigid structures must be freed so that it can interact with other information. If only relevant information is going to be accepted, then chance processes are not able to produce new ideas. To seek out only relevant information is to attempt to assess the full usefulness of that information even before it has been examined. Relevance must refer to some established idea, and information gathered with this in mind can only tend to support that idea. It is useless to try to develop a new idea by considering only the information that was relevant to the old one. By definition relevance implies preconceived ideas.

Ideally the mind should be allowed to accept information haphazardly from any source. This information is not sorted or filed under different headings but is allowed free interaction. Attention flits rapidly over the whole field, observing but not organizing, pausing long enough with an emerging idea to follow its development but not long enough to force it into a relevant mould. Ideally the mind should become an open house to information, a place where everything is welcomed, not only the invited or interesting guests but also the casual strangers or gate-crashers.

In practice the attitude described above is impossible. The amount of available information grows at such a terrific rate that the total mass of printed words doubles itself every ten years. Even in one field the amount of highly relevant information is so huge that there is little chance of covering it all even with sophisticated computer search methods. The only way out seems to make the field of interest smaller and smaller through increasing specialization. Under these conditions an order of relevance has to be used: there is the most relevant information, followed by the less relevant, and so on. One ends up with the same effect as vertical thinking which only follows the highest probabilities. As a result there is little hope of new ideas coming about through the acceptance of information from another field.

The dilemma is very real. When one comes to the end of an article in a scientific journal the following article always seems highly relevant. Any medical journal picked up at random can always be found to contain one or two papers of apparently high relevance. When I was at Harvard I used to make a habit of picking up at random a journal from the display shelf at the entrance to the library. There was never a time when a journal selected in this manner did not contain at least one useful article. If such a random selection produced this result, it is frightening to think what a complete search would reveal. Unfortunately the matter gets worse as one goes more deeply into a subject. As the ideas grow more and more basic, the inter-relationships with both fields become more obvious; instead of narrowing, the field of relevance becomes even wider.

Pasteur covered many fields. He investigated spontaneous generation of life, the fermentation of wines, silk-worm disease, chicken cholera, anthrax and rabies (for which he produced effective preventative methods), and many other subjects. On each occasion there seemed to be chance events that favoured Pasteur. One of his assistants was careless about a culture of chicken-cholera germs and the culture lost its power to cause the disease. But Pasteur noticed that this weakened culture actually protected the chickens to which it had been given against infection with a virulent culture. Thus the very important idea of protection by inoculation of germs of weakened virulence came about. In his early work on tartaric acid Pasteur noticed that a solution which had become fermented by accident contained only one sort of tartaric acid, the other sort having been consumed by the fermenting organisms. This led to a method for separating the two sorts, an added insight into the nature of tartaric acid and an increased interest in fermentation, which was to lead Pasteur to improve the existing methods of making both wine and beer. Observation of the behaviour of earthworms on a farm infected with anthrax suggested to Pasteur how infection could be brought from the buried corpse to the healthy animals grazing above. Pasteur himself was perfectly willing to acknowledge the contributions of chance, but pointed out that it is the readiness of the mind to develop these contributions that matters.

The mind that makes most of the opportunities offered by chance may be likened to a mechanic who is so gifted that he can make almost any car work. It would be unfair to envy him his good fortune in always finding cars in good working order.

With practice in looking at things in different ways the capacity to find a context for any given bit of information increases to a remarkable extent. As one gets better at lateral thinking, chance offerings of information, chance conjunctions of ideas, come to be more and more useful. It is not that chance itself has changed, but simply that one gets better at harvesting it.

A useful technique that sometimes helps towards the formation of new ideas or new ways of looking at things is to pick an object out of the environment and then try to see how it could be relevant to the matter under consideration. The supposition is that if both the object and the problem are simultaneously held in consciousness, some sort of context will gradually develop to embrace them both. The selected object may prove relevant by offering a new way of looking at things; by suggesting a novel type of relationship or principle; as a link to some other and more pertinent matter; as a line of thought to be avoided. Meaning is not something that lies within an object but a description of the way the object affects the mind, the way it brings about or fits into a pattern of thought. This pattern of thought may already exist or it may swiftly grow around the object to give it a context and therefore a meaning.

The sheer impossibility of covering all relevant material paradoxically makes it more necessary than ever to rely on chance encounters for new influences.

The ability to concentrate on a problem to the exclusion of all other matters is usually taken to be a virtue. Isolated by the power of concentration, a problem is expected to solve itself. Chance influences are excluded as much as possible. This procedure effectively prevents the formation of new ideas, for any outside influence which could lead to a new way of treating the problem is deliberately excluded. Concentration on the problem only serves to reinforce the rigid way it is being considered at the moment.

A well-known way of alleviating the sterility of concentration is to break off periodically to consider some other matter which has nothing to do with the main problem. However, it is much more effective to allow outside influences to come in and alter the rigidity of a way of looking at things while the problem is actually being examined. The first way merely allows one to get out of a rut, the second way may force one out of the rut and lead one on to something different.

The use of chance is passive but watchful. It is not easy deliberately to remove deliberation from a process. It is not easy to make a conscious effort to avoid conscious effort. At first waiting for something to turn up by chance may seem a doubtful business. The very definition of chance suggests that nothing may turn up, and the temptation to organize some line of thought is strong. It is necessary to survive the temptation and to be confident that if waiting is sufficiently passive, then something will always turn up, usually not one thing but too many things. Initially the disinclination to settle on some line of thought will lead to a great restlessness and a search for distractions, but as skill in the use of lateral thinking increases, then ideas start to turn up. Confidence grows, and as it grows, thinking without consciously directing thought becomes easier; as it becomes easier it becomes more effective.

8

Reading about lateral thinking is nearly as awkward as writing about it and both are much less real than the actual use of lateral thinking. Describing the process in abstract terms makes it seem vague and removes all the vividness and vigour that are part of a practical process. Descriptions of the process tend either to be obscure (and hence impressive) or else obvious and even tautologous. Unfortunately the obviousness of a principle when it is real as a description is not carried over to ease of application of that principle in a practical setting.

The practical application of lateral thinking is of more use than the philosophical possibility, and therefore the best way to describe lateral processes is to show them in action. It is possible to do this by analysing in detail the thought processes behind great new ideas in history. Such descriptive analysis is not, however, very satisfactory. The analysis has to be second-hand and would depend on the recorded thoughts of those who had the new ideas. These thoughts are usually recorded after the idea has come about, sometimes a very long time after. The recording may not be done by the originator of the idea, but by some admiring disciple. Using hindsight from a position of success it is very easy to rationalize the way an idea actually came about. There is a tendency to select some details and ignore others, until the whole process seems a more fitting approach to the successful finale. The falsification need not be deliberate, but it remains a description from a special point of view. Not all scientists are as honest as Pasteur was and quite often the contributions of chance are ignored while the careful deliberations of logic are emphasized. Vertical thinking is the respectable way to arrive at an idea, and in looking back it is not difficult to provide a logical structure for what really came about in other ways.

The alternative to such second-hand description is to try to observe at first hand the way lateral processes bring about new ideas. This chapter contains brief descriptions of the way some ideas came about. The examples are not of any particular importance and they are chosen only because they illustrate some point or other about lateral thinking. For this reason the descriptions are not detailed but merely indicate the lateral point. This catalogue of examples, chosen out of the many that occurred over the three years during which the concept of lateral thinking developed, is certainly not meant to indicate what can be done with lateral thinking. The examples are much too trivial for that. The problems were simply opportunities to watch in one's own mind the processes by which a new idea was formed. As a spectator of these processes one cannot claim any more credit than a theatre audience can claim credit for a play which fascinates it.

In all the examples the major considerations were simplicity and effectiveness, the two aims of lateral thinking. It would be nice to suppose that the striving for simplicity was an attempt to reverse the trend towards ever-increasing complexity, but in fact it was as much dictated by laziness and lack of technical skill. The examples used are neither simple ways of doing things or simple mechanical devices. Gadgets are a very lowly form of intellectual achievement, but they do have a convenient completeness: there is a beginning, a middle and an end.

The test was well known and simple, but the equipment required was so bulky that it had to be wheeled around on a large trolley. There seemed a need for a device small enough to be slipped into the pocket. The bulky equipment consisted of an electronic pressure-measuring device with its amplifier, and a recorder to make a record of the changes in the blood pressure within the artery when the patient performed a certain breathing test. From the pattern of change in the blood pressure it was possible to detect the onset of heart failure. The first stage in the development of a new device was to get away from the idea that a recording was essential. Since the pattern of change was all that was used it seemed possible that this could be appreciated as it was taking place. The next dominant idea to be avoided was the notion of turning the pressure changes into an electrical current which could be amplified to give a precision quite superfluous for this purpose. The most direct way of making the pressure changes visible would be the well-known one of seeing how high a column of liquid could be supported by the pressure. Unfortunately, the column would have to be so high that this method would have been impossibly cumbersome. Nor would it have worked well, for the inertia of the large bulk of fluid required would have made it difficult to reproduce the beat-to-beat pressure changes within the artery. At this point the further development of the device depended on the happy conjunction of two ideas. One was that of an ordinary clinical thermometer, and the decision that the device would have to be as simple as that. The other was a memory from about ten years previously of a routine (external) blood-pressure-measuring device which had used a much shorter column of mercury than usual by closing the end of the tube so that the rising mercury column had to compress the air before it. The thin capillary tube in the thermometer, the bulb at the end and the miniature column that could be used if the tube end was closed, all came together to give a glass device about as big as a thermometer which proved to be quite accurate enough for this particular test.

The device was still inconvenient to prepare for each test, and it was also awkward to make, as it involved some tricky glass-blowing. The next stage in the development of the idea came about when someone asked for yet another of these devices. There happened to be a roll of thin nylon tubing lying on the desk and immediately the idea of using a short length of this as a disposable device, instead of the glass one, came to mind. In the end a device about the size of a short piece of string and costing about one shilling replaced (for this particular test only) the bulky apparatus which cost about a thousand pounds. In this example the development of the idea depended on getting away from preconceived notions, a reluctance to abandon a principle that at first seemed unsuitable, a fortunate memory and especially the stimulating effect of an unrelated object.

The stimulating effect of a casually encountered object is also well shown in the example of the currency converter. This was to be a simple plastic device that would enable shoppers abroad to convert quickly the foreign price tag into the home equivalent. Many possible designs were visualized, but all were too finicky or too elaborate. The final design was suggested that evening by the flattened 'X' symbol on the bottom of the British Railways dining-car bill. This symbol, regarded not as an 'X' but as two 'Vs' placed apex to apex, suggested a nomogram, and this was the basis of the final design which followed after a few doodles with a ball-point on the back of the bill. A nomogram is a perfectly straightforward way of dealing with proportional conversions and it could certainly have been reached by vertical thinking, but it was not.

In the same way a search for a simple way of making visible in slow motion the behaviour of waves travelling along a line ended with a collection of those brightly coloured glass balls that hang on Christmas trees. It was Christmas time and the insistent presence of these baubles gave rise to the idea of using them as a series of linked pendulums with energy transfer in slow motion from one to another on a resonance basis.

The way in which an unsought-for stimulus can set off a useful train of ideas was deliberately made use of in the design of a simple device to test lung function. There are many excellent devices available for this purpose, but the idea was to see if something much simpler and cheaper could be developed. Woolworth's was deliberately used as a setting full of the sort of objects which might trigger off an idea. There were no preconceived ideas. It was just a matter of wandering around until something suggested itself. The first things to excite attention were some plastic flutes. These led quickly to an idea for a device that made a noise as the patient blew through it, and in this context a toy plastic concertina suggested itself as a source of a small noise-making reed. From the plastic flute came the idea of a tube with holes down the side and a whistle at the far end. An estimation of the speed of the air leaving the lungs might be obtained by seeing how many side holes could be uncovered before it became impossible to sound the whistle. This idea did not work, but it did provide a means of getting away from the dominant idea of moving vanes and dial-indicators which were the basis of the current equipment. The basic idea of producing a noise under different degrees of difficulty as an index of lung function was set off. The advantage of the idea was its simplicity and especially the lack of any moving parts to go wrong. The next stage was simply to reverse the position of the whistle and the leak-holes: the whistle was to be put at the side of the tube and the variable leak-hole at the end. A device along these lines made use of the tiny reed from the toy concertina, but there was trouble with the variable leak-hole which could not be made both simple and robust. Out of this difficulty came the idea of doing away with a variable leak-hole and having instead several fixed leak-holes of differing sizes. This arrangement seemed quite satisfactory. One day, in the course of casual playing around, the reed in the side of the tube was covered with a finger and, unexpectedly, the device still produced a noise when it was blown through. It soon became obvious that a fortunate choice of shape for the end-hole was providing a natural whistle. A selection of different sizes of end-hole gave a range of very simple devices consisting of ordinary plastic tubes closed at one end by plates with circular holes in them. In order to get a whistling sound it was necessary to blow with a certain strength and in this way the velocity of the air could be estimated by seeing which of the tubes could be made to whistle. The problem seemed to have been solved in a surprisingly easy way. There was, however, a snag in that if one blew too hard, sometimes no whistle would be sounded with a tube which should have given a whistle.

The next stage in the development of the idea involved discarding all that had been achieved. One morning while breakfast was being cooked the whistle from a whistling kettle suddenly became obvious as the basis of a new version of the device. Attached by sticky tape to a cardboard tube that had once contained a rolled silk calendar, the whistle from the kettle was incorporated in a prototype. In the side of the tube, slots were cut with a razor blade; as more and more of this side slot was occluded with the fingers it became progressively easier to sound the whistle. With very little alteration this design formed the basis of the final whistle in which the slot was occluded by sliding the plastic whistle tube in and out of the disposable cardboard mouthpiece. In this example the final design was much closer to the first.

The L-game is a good example of the usefulness of playing around coupled with a very rigid idea of what the final result should be. A dinner-table conversation at Trinity College,

Cambridge, had touched on the difficulty of getting a computer to play good chess on account of the great number of playing pieces and hence the vast number of possible moves. It seemed amusing to try to devise a board game that would be as simple as possible and yet interesting enough to be played with skill. The next morning a square piece of plastic found in a jacket pocket provided the focus for random playing around that led to a large number of possible ideas. Since there was no easy way of telling which idea would make a good game, the only way to assess each idea was to try to find one reason why it would not make a good game, and to try it out in the pub. In a purely random manner the game evolved into the L-game. This was intended to be the simplest possible game of skill. Each player has a single (L-shaped) piece which he manoeuvres in a small squared board so as to trap the other player's piece. There are also two neutral pieces. Since there are over eighteen thousand playing positions the game can be played with a high degree of skill, yet it is simpler to learn than noughts and crosses. In this case the playing around was beautifully free and undirected since there was no necessity to devise anything at all and the only consideration was simplicity.

The difficulty with playing around with no apparent purpose is that it often seems unrewarding at the time; one cannot appreciate that it may pay dividends later. One particular experiment on the renal circulation seemed to require elaborate equipment and special arrangements of the perfusing system. In the end it turned out that an experiment could be performed quite simply with only a finger as the most important piece of apparatus. The aim was to increase the blood pressure at a certain point within the kidney by decreasing the outflow (intermittently) instead of by increasing the inflow as was usually done. The idea was suggested by a good deal of messing around with water and tubes that had taken place two years before in another context. A more interesting point about this example is that an almost similar experiment (but with constant diminution of outflow) was known not to work. Had this knowledge been available at the time, this particular experiment would probably never have been done; and yet it worked.

In many of the above examples an unsought stimulus has set off a useful train of thought. Instead of waiting for such a chance encounter or deliberately exposing oneself to a collection of random stimuli, it is possible consciously to pick on some feature in the environment and to stay with it until it demonstrates a relevance to the problem in hand. The object must be chosen quite at random; there is no usefulness in choosing an object that already seems relevant. When the problem was to immobilize a car so that it could not be driven away by someone with a duplicate key, the object on which attention was fixed was an ordinary pin. After a few minutes the pin developed a relevance to the problem: the solution was to insert the pin into the lock so that no key would fit. In due course the pin was extracted with a magnet.

The same deliberate process took place when the problem, presented as an inventing challenge by a magazine, was to design a simple device that would climb up walls and go along the ceiling. A preliminary version of this device (called Suzie, a sister to Freddie who will be met later) performed quite satisfactorily, but one morning in the bathroom the toilet roll was picked out as an object of fixation that was required to show a relevance to the problem. The contribution of the toilet roll was the suggestion of a spiral which eventually became transformed into a particularly effective method of attaching the adhesive tyres to the device, so that as it rolled up the wall, instead of falling off, it stuck itself on ever more firmly.

A rather more complicated process lay behind the design of some mechanical hands to help in experimental procedures. The requirement was for a mechanical holding device which would be flexible enough to be easily moulded into shape and then be capable of instantly becoming rigid enough to carry out its holding function. Mechanical devices which are placed in position and then screwed into immobility are a bother and rarely adaptable enough. The basic friction idea of the screw devices was, however, reverted to after several other principles, such as magnetism, had been rejected. On this occasion a strip of chromatography paper (similar to blotting paper) which was lying around was fixed upon. Clearly the paper had sufficient flexibility to be easily moulded around an object, but it would have no rigidity to hold the object. A number of layers of the paper could be made fairly rigid if only they could be pressed together tightly enough for any attempted movement to encounter high friction between them. The difficulty was to leave the layers loose enough in the beginning for the device to be flexible and then rapidly press them tightly together to give rigidity. The problem seemed impossible until by deliberate reversal of the situation the idea of pulling them together was considered. At once it became obvious that the strips could be pulled together by suction. All that was needed was to place strips of the paper in a thin rubber tube sealed at one end and connected to suction at the other. As soon as suction was applied, the paper strips became pressed firmly together, and from being completely flexible (in one plane), the structure became quite rigid. A comparable device which was flexible in more than one plane was subsequently developed, using the same principles.

A challenge issued on a country walk involved using some chicken wire as the stimulus to devise an indoor game. A lot of playing around with hexagon shapes did not turn up anything useful. Many months later an urgent request to devise some games for a magazine, coupled with the casual observation of a wire-lattice litter bin, revived the hexagon idea but in an immediately useful way. At the same time the very same litter bin gave rise to an idea for a completely different game which was also published by the magazine. The lattice-work of the litter bin suggested pathways that branched and rejoined. Such pathways formed the basis of a game in which each player sought to reach a goal ahead of the other players by anticipating their choice of pathway at each move while disguising his own. Victory in this game depends on making a sequence of correct assessments of the other players' intentions.

It is sometimes curious how two quite different problems may be solved almost simultaneously. The idea for the 'T' shapes used in a previous chapter came during a period of doodling in one of those cantilevered steel frame chairs. Almost simultaneously came the idea of using the springiness of the chair for a device to test some aspects of heart function. It is a very well-known fact that with each heart beat the body recoils slightly, and this phenomenon can be seen in the oscillations of the pointer on good weighing machines. For a device making use of this principle the office chair turned out to be far more suitable than many of the other heavily engineered devices that had been considered in the previous months. The patient sits on the chair and each time his heart beats his body recoils proportionately and the seat of the chair is depressed very slightly. By means of a clutch mechanism (originally made of a curtain hook, a bit of fishing line, plasticine and a syringe), the chair is connected to a sensing device which picks up the tiny movements and displays them on paper as a pattern which tells something about heart function. When the clutch is disconnected, even violent movements of the chair do not harm the delicate sensing device. In this case a great deal of deliberate effort had failed to provide an idea as simple as that which arrived by itself.

Quite often the difficulty in looking for something is that one carries in mind not the principle itself but some particular embodiment of it. It can be an amusing exercise to try to find examples of some particular thing that is needed to try out an idea. One day a search for a small paraboloid surface ended up with the purchase from Woolworth's of a plastic egg-cup which provided a most suitable shape. On another occasion the search for some sort of mesh that would break up the foam in a bubble-oxygenerator ended up with the following collection of objects: a washing-up brush, a nylon pot-scourer, a plastic lattice flower-pot cover, hair-curlers, nylon briefs, and finally nylon stockings borrowed as an afterthought from a secretary. The pot-scourer proved best.

In itself the choice of simple objects has no virtue at all over more sophisticated methods which usually work better; the only advantage is that the simple objects are more easily available, and there is always a certain impatience to try out an idea to see if it works in principle before going on to refinement later.

Sometimes it is amusing just to look at an object and try to develop an idea from it. This time it is not a question of seeing how the object can be related to a particular problem, it is just a matter of mental playing around. At dinner one evening a train of thought connected the wine bottle on the table to the cutlery. From this arose an amusing problem to do with the arranging of knives on the top of a bottle. The form of the idea may have had something to do with the presence of an architect. The bottles and knives were left lying around overnight. In the morning a little more playing around produced a further development of the idea which was then written up into a book over the week-end (*The Five-day Course in Thinking*).

On another occasion the sight of some brightly coloured toy balloons in a drugstore developed into a method of working out a problem that involved complicated system interactions. The problem was at the time being programmed for consumption by an electronic computer because this had seemed the only way to tackle it. The ten-cent packet of balloons, however, led to a model for studying the basic principles of the matter, and the two and a half million dollar computer became superfluous. (The computer time would actually only have amounted to a few hundred dollars and the solution would have had an exactness I did not require.)

Depending on the particular approach used, problems may be simple to work out or much more complicated. One Sunday afternoon the sight of someone smoking led to the mental exercise of considering what could be done about the cigarette problem. The two obvious approaches were to try to remove harmful substances from cigarettes, or to get people to smoke less. A naive approach to the first part of the problem would involve filtering out some of the tar particles from the inhaled smoke. (A more sophisticated approach would involve trying to alter the chemical composition or combustion so that such substances were not formed.) Reversing this idea one could also lower the concentration of smoke particles by adding something to the smoke instead of taking something out. Pin-holes in the cigarette would allow air to be drawn in and the smoke diluted. This led on to an idea for trying to wean people from cigarettes by progressively weakening the taste as the number of pin-holes was increased. In order to see how the cigarettes would burn with pin-holes in them a crude preliminary test made use of a vacuum cleaner as a smoking machine.

The usefulness of ordinary everyday objects when looked at in the light of some special requirement is often surprising. On another occasion a source of high-pressure gas which could be released by pressure on a trigger was needed. This was to do with a personal defensive weapon that arose out of the inventing challenge mentioned earlier. The soda-siphon sitting on the drinks tray was the obvious answer, it was only necessary to envisage it empty of liquid and then the high-pressure gas and the convenient trigger were provided. Thinking of a soda-siphon only as something to do with drinks or something to squirt water out of would not have led to this idea, but the physical presence of the soda-siphon made it possible to break out of the usual classification.

One of the devices which was most fun to design was Freddie the space-age pet. The idea was to have a pet suitable for modern living: the animal was to provide intelligent animation and yet not require feeding, taking out, or otherwise looking after. The aim was a smooth black sphere that rolled about on its own; whenever it came up against an object it would nonchalantly roll off in a different direction; if it went down a cul-de-sac it would simply roll out again. This creature was particularly amusing to design because all sorts of complicated ways of doing it were considered, but the final mechanism turned out to be very simple and made use of a pencil, an eraser, a ball-point pen and a toy electric car. There was some difficulty in finding a suitable sphere and one attempt at making one involved blowing up a balloon, covering it with papier-mâché strips and then bursting the balloon. But in the end a suitable sphere was casually encountered in a shop window on Lexington Avenue, New York, as part of a child's toy.

Many of the examples given could perfectly well have been worked out as adequately, or better, by careful logical deliberations. The interesting point is whether they would actually have been worked out in this way. Many of the ideas were triggered off or advanced further by things which were not actively looked for. It is easy to say that this process was a roundabout way of achieving something that could have been done more directly by logic. But logic needs a direction in which to work. Many of the ideas came about precisely because there was no commitment to a fixed way of doing things. As in other instances of the use of lateral thinking, it is always possible to rationalize once the result has been achieved. Many of the devices have not been described in full and those who would like to fill in the details logically for their own amusement are invited to do so. What was of interest was the process, not the product. Those who cannot distinguish between the two and do not accept the relevance of gadgets would no doubt have scorned the way Einstein often amused himself in this manner.

9

The last chapter may have given the impression that the chief usefulness of lateral thinking lies in the invention or design of mechanical gadgets. It may be felt that, interesting as these devices might be, they do not play a significant role in everyday affairs and that the desire to create devices of this nature is strictly limited. As pointed out before, the actual devices themselves are of no importance at all; they are merely the most convenient way to show the processes of lateral thinking in action.

The use of scientific ideas as illustrations of the way new ideas come about may also have given the impression that lateral thinking is only for those who are engaged in research work. Since the majority of people are neither engaged in research work nor interested in inventing, lateral thinking would seem to be a luxury which can be done without. This would be a mistake, for the way of thinking illustrated with the scientific ideas or simple inventions can just as simply be applied to other situations. The process is a basic one. The mother who put her child in a play-pen to stop him pulling the Christmas tree to bits was using one sort of thinking; the husband who decided it made more sense to put the tree into the play-pen instead was using another sort of thinking. From personal experience everyone can pick out isolated instances of lateral thinking which have been very useful at the time.

On the very day that the idea of using balloons to help

work out a problem instead of the large computer occurred to me, I was given a lesson in the narrowness of vertical thinking. I had lent my apartment to a friend for the week-end and when I got back I found that the reading lamp would not work. I made sure that it was properly plugged in, I changed the bulb, checked the fuse and even got as far as dismantling the plug. It was only after all this vertical effort that I suddenly realized that my friend, unaware of my habits, had switched off the light at the wall switch instead of using the switch on the lamp base as I always did. Because my attention was concentrated on the lamp and because I proceeded vertically from that point, I made a problem of what was really a simple situation. Had I shifted my attention from the lamp itself to other factors, such as my friend, there would have been no problem.

It is only too easy to be led along the path of highest probability. One may be prepared to forego the benefits of lateral thinking on the grounds that one is not interested in having new ideas; but is one prepared to accept the restrictions of vertical thinking? New ideas are the positive aspect of lateral thinking, but those who never use lateral thinking do not simply forego this positive aspect – they also incur a definite disadvantage. This disadvantage is the way such people can be manipulated, for their minds always follow a predictable high-probability pathway.

In ju-jitsu one takes advantage of the predictable direction of an attack to turn the opponent's strength and weight against himself. In the same way the predictable workings of the mind of a vertical thinker can also be taken advantage of. This process is very effectively used by stage magicians. All stage tricks, except those that depend on machinery or sleight of hand, use the principle of leading the audience along the high-probability of thinking. The great Houdini used to challenge the audience to provide a lock to secure about his wrists a pair of handcuffs. When the handcuffs had been securely fastened Houdini would be put into a sack and a few moments later would appear freed of the handcuffs. One way of effecting this escape was to have a special pin in the hinge of the handcuffs. This pin could only be extracted with a magnet and once it was extracted the handcuffs fell open. While everyone's attention was directed to the excellence of the lock, Houdini simply undid the hinge and then did it up again.

The same basic principle was used by Houdini in his sawing-the-lady-in-half presentation. A girl would get into the empty box on the stage and then the box would be suspended above the stage, so that no one could enter or leave. When the box had been raised off the stage, Houdini would open the top end to show the girl's head and then the bottom end to show her feet. The box would then be sawn in half but the girl would emerge unscathed. Vertical thinkers were puzzled because no one could enter or leave the suspended box and clearly the girl was in it at the start of the sawing. In fact the trick had been completed before the box had ever left the floor of the stage – before the vertical thinkers had even started to think. The box was placed over a trap-door in the stage, and as soon as the audience had examined it a girl entered it from below. The head and feet shown by Houdini after the box was suspended belonged to two different girls between whom the saw passed.

Another of Houdini's stage tricks involved a girl who was carried on to the stage by four turbaned Indians, one at each corner of the plate-glass sheet on which she was reclining. Houdini then threw a sheet over the girl and when he whisked it away she had disappeared. The explanation was that one of the four Indians who were taken for granted as helpers was not a person at all, but a hollow dummy into which the girl slithered and inside which she walked off the stage.

These tricks are obvious once they are explained, but in

their day they were effective, especially when accompanied by the patter of the stage magician who encouraged the audience along that path of high-probability thinking which they were so keen to take. To appreciate what was really being done, it was necessary to take a low-probability side-turning off the highway of high probability. Once such a turning was missed, there was no chance of getting back to it through vertical thinking.

Stage magic creates a very artificial situation, but it does show quite clearly how easy it is to take advantage of people who use only high-probability or vertical thinking. Con-men, salesmen, politicians and professional persuaders of every sort would be very nearly out of business if it was not more natural for the mind to use vertical thinking than lateral thinking. Their success is determined by how good they are at pointing out the high-probability path that suits their purpose – by suitable emphasis they can create a high-probability path where one did not exist before. (In this context it would not be very useful to define a high-probability path as the path which most people would eventually take, for that would be a circular definition. High probability is defined on a functional, neurological level as the more marked facilitation of one pathway brought about by familiarity and modified by the motivation of the moment.) Experience cannot be easily altered, but by manipulating motivation probabilities can be effectively changed.

The people who tend to use lateral thinking most naturally in their work are journalists and advertising people, who develop the faculty for looking at things in different ways. Among the most rigid vertical thinkers are lawyers, doctors and to some extent business people, all of whom prefer things to be rigid, defined, and orthodox, for it is only then that they can bring to bear their experience and technical training.

It might be wondered where the artist comes in. In his search for new ways of looking at things, in his dedication to breaking down the old conventions of perception, is not the artist the supreme user of lateral thinking? In the world of art it would seem that lateral thinking is going on all the time under the more self-satisfying name of creative thinking. The artist is open to ideas, influences and chance. The artist seeks to develop an intense awareness. The artist tries to escape from the accepted vision of things often by deliberate use of unreason. The cult of psychedelic experience is a deliberate attempt to heighten awareness in order to find more significant ways of looking at things. Are not all these the very essence of lateral thinking?

The trouble with creative thinking in art is that it is so easy to stop halfway. Indeed, the less talented have no choice. Escape from the old ideas becomes a virtue in itself. Originality is all. There is an enthusiasm to step down from the limitations of accepted order into the limitless potential of chaos, but too often this step is regarded as an achievement in itself rather than only the first stage towards achievement. The true purpose of lateral thinking is not to wallow in formless chaos but to emerge from it with an effective new idea. The new idea is likely to have a classic simplicity of form; it is likely to have an orderliness which is far from the formlessness of the chaos from which it emerged.

The ideal aimed at in lateral thinking is the simplicity of extreme sophistication, the simplicity of an idea that is very effective in action and yet elemental in its form. It is the simplicity of richness, not of poverty. It is the simplicity of fullness, not of emptiness.

With art, because there is no objective end-point, it seems too easy to stop at the chaos stage and get no further. An inventor who produces impossible inventions that do not work expects little credit because he has not reached the effective stage. But how is an artist to know when he is wallowing in free form and when he has reached an effective re-synthesis? There are no objective criteria, and subjective judgement is difficult as it is given either by those who are unable to escape from the old expectations or by those to whom escape is an end in itself.

In the above context it is inevitable that weirdness for its own sake must flourish. The grotesque and the bizarre are the most elementary forms of newness and the most facile to achieve. A really new idea never seems bizarre because it has an independence and completeness of its own. Bizarre ideas are not new but simply distortions of the old. Deliberate distortion of an old idea as a technique to achieve a new one was suggested earlier, but it is only a technique, not an achievement. The first motor-cars used distortions of the carriage design, and even today there has been no radical new design. Distortion of this sort is of course perfectly justified in the hope that it may gradually mature into a new idea, but it is another matter when distortion presumes to be treated as a new idea.

If you put a pebble into one of the cylinders of a beautifully running car engine you will get some weird and wonderfully original noises. One attitude of mind would be to stand around marvelling at the wonderful noises of destruction. The other attitude would be to use the noise to stimulate new ideas, either to do with the engine (for instance, an engine without cylinders), or in terms of pure sound, or in some other context. It is no fault of the artist that the first attitude is so easy to mistake for the second in the world of art. True creative thinking can be an especially talented form of lateral thinking, but spurious creative thinking is another matter.

In a way, science is a superior form of art, since the beauty of a new idea is no longer a matter of opinion or fashion. Science lacks emotional involvement and universal appeal, but it has an intrinsic rightness. The difference between the requirements of art and science is charmingly shown in the work of Leonardo da Vinci. About the beauty of da Vinci's art there would seem to be no disagreement. His scientific ideas, however, often showed only the artistic type of beauty. In a sketch of his proposed flying machine da Vinci was more concerned with making adequate provision for the pilot to step to the ground than with the ability of the machine to fly. He was more concerned with the completeness of what could be appreciated than with the possibility of what could not.

Most scientists could learn much about lateral thinking from artists, but many artists would be most uncomfortable if they had to follow lateral thinking through to its proper end. Those people who feel that the artist's way of life, in its caricature form, would be the fullest possible expression of the lateral way of thinking have completely misunderstood the nature of the process. Lateral thinking does seek to escape from the dominance of rigid and accepted ways of looking at things: but the purpose of the escape is a new and simpler order, not disorder. Disorder is only a means of escape, not a destination. However, lateral thinking would be of little use if all it brought about was a new order in exchange for the old one. Lateral thinking is concerned with finding new, simpler, and more effective ideas, but it is even more concerned with the fluidity which allows one idea to be exchanged for a better one, and then for an even better one, and so on.

Even if one is perfectly content with a particular way of looking at things, there is amusement to be had in finding another way to look at them now and again. Humour has much to do with lateral thinking. Humour occurs when the most probable way of looking at things is disrupted by a sudden appreciation that there is another way of looking at them. The first way still remains the high-probability way, there is no sudden switch over as there is with an 'eureka moment' when the new way of looking at things at once becomes the new high-probability way. With humour the mind switches back and forth between the obvious way of looking at things and the unexpected, but plausible, way. It is this oscillation that is peculiar to the lateral thinking of humour. The effect of the oscillation also depends much on the motivation involved, hence the success of sex humour.

A funny man in conversation or on the stage will seem to get funnier and funnier as he carries his audience with him. The audience becomes better and better at detecting the alternative ways of looking at things and also more ready to accept the alternative ways supplied by the funny man.

Anyone with a good sense of humour ought to be able to understand the nature of lateral thinking much better than someone without.

10

The aim of lateral thinking is to generate new ideas. But is anyone really interested in new ideas apart from the person who has them? It is a myth that those who are in a position to do something about new ideas are eagerly awaiting them. And there is no reason why it should be otherwise, for it is easy enough to have a new idea but much more difficult to put it into effect. In general there is an enthusiasm for the idea of having new ideas, but not for the new ideas themselves. A common attitude resembles that of the man who thanked God the sun had gone in and he did not have to go out and enjoy it.

No one is interested in new ideas as such but only in effective new ideas. The effectiveness of a new idea depends not so much on the idea itself as on the ability of the person who is judging it. Where success or failure of an idea has a real value in terms of cash or pride, there is much incentive to make a sound judgement. Unfortunately past experience is the best basis for a sound judgement, and by definition new ideas cannot always be judged on the basis of past experience. Inertia thinking is a reluctance to leave the past, momentum thinking is an eagerness to continue the past forward into the future; both policies make good sense but they do not make the maximum use of new ideas. Fear of wasting money on a new idea is often overcome only by fear of losing money through a competitor adopting the idea. Ideally a manufacturer would like to be second in the field; not so far behind that the market is saturated, but far enough behind to be able to evaluate the success of the idea. This phenomenon was shown with the development of the fibre-tip pen which was first marketed by a Japanese firm and then rapidly followed by everyone else.

Reluctance to take on a new idea is coupled with the assumption that if the idea is really good enough it will win through in the end. For years no one was interested in the basic idea behind the extraordinarily successful Xerox copying machine. When Walter Hunt and Elias Howe invented the sewing machine, no one had any faith in its future. 'Monopoly', the most successful of all modern games, was thoroughly rejected at first by the manufacturers who subsequently made a fortune from it. One can easily point to the good ideas that made it in the end, but not to the ones that disappeared, for they are lost.

Reluctance to greet new ideas is no more than reluctance to invest money in new ideas, reluctance to risk large sums of money on something that cannot be effectively judged until it has come about. The use of lateral thinking is not, however, confined to the development of new products, but extends to all fields in which new ways of looking at things can be helpful. New ideas do not only mean spending money, more often they mean saving money. A more efficient way of doing things, a use for waste material, an improved design which is simpler to make and less liable to faulty assembly, the way the cost of something can be reduced without affecting its function – these are all fields where new ideas can save money. Lateral thinking is not only concerned with the research and development side but also with organization and methods, value analysis and operational research. Each of these fields has its own carefully honed techniques and its own fund of experience to serve it, but the basic principle of effective analysis and new ideas is common to all of them.

Few ways of doing things are beyond improvement in terms of efficiency and cost. Effective analysis and recognized techniques can bring about a great improvement; a new idea can carry that improvement still further. There is no limit to the effect a new idea may have; it may save a few pounds or millions of pounds. Quite recently an industrialist told me how a bright new idea in the middle of the night cost the firm concerned more than ten million pounds to implement, but saved them more than one hundred million pounds.

At no point in orthodox education are lateral thinking habits developed. The capacity to generate new ideas remains a matter of a natural aptitude that has survived the long years of vertical thinking. Yet some proficiency in lateral thinking would be of use to everyone who needs new ideas. A common attitude is to assume that new ideas are the business of the research department alone. One has only to set up a research department to relieve oneself of the necessity to have new ideas. But the best research department is of little use if its ideas are never adopted; a poor research department is improved if its ideas are amplified, and hence an awareness of lateral thinking must be useful to general management.

In an atomic pile a chain reaction comes about when a particle splits off from one atom nucleus and then collides with another atom nucleus and dislodges a second particle which in turn collides with a second nucleus. If the mass of material is large enough, the chain reaction becomes an explosion. So it is with ideas. One new idea can set off a second new idea in the same mind or in another, and a sort of chain reaction follows. (This effect is often seen with a radical new discovery in science.) In an atomic pile an explosion is prevented by inserting rods of cadmium which mop up the particles which are shooting around. In this way the energy in the pile is controlled. If there are too many rods, the chain reaction stops and the pile can no longer produce any energy. People who are unable to appreciate new ideas are like the rods: some of them are necessary to prevent a destructive explosion, but too many make it impossible for the pile to produce any energy.

There is no reason why lateral thinking habits should not be acquired. Just as one acquires skill in golf or skiing or foreign languages, so one can gradually acquire a facility in lateral thinking. As with golf or skiing, however, one does not become an expert simply by reading about it. There is no magic formula which, once learned, can thereafter be applied with great effectiveness. It is true that there are specific techniques which can be used and these are suggested in other chapters, but lateral thinking is more a habit of mind than knowledge of some technique. This habit can be acquired by specific training and it should be possible to do this in a deliberate manner. As in golf, a sort of general coaching would be of some use, but of much more use would be individual attention to find out in any one person the particular difficulties that interfered with the fluency of the process.

The fanatic is effective because he sees everything according to a rigid pattern. The absolute commitment to this pattern provides a definite direction for his actions and firm standards with which to judge results. By excluding the possibility of there being any alternative way of looking at things, the fanatic excludes doubt and indecision. It may be felt that the habit of trying to look at things in different ways would lessen the effectiveness of those who felt that the rapidity of a decision was of more importance than its nature. Even if this attitude towards decisions was acceptable and not just an excuse for an inability to make the necessary considerations, there would be little danger that lateral thinking habits would interfere. A person with a particular type of mind would never find that this had been radically changed by the acquisition of some skill in lateral thinking; such skill would be a bonus.

It is not easy to get outside a particular way of looking at things in order to find a new way. Very often all the basic ingredients of a new idea are already to hand and all that is required is a particular way of assembling them. The aim of the lateral thinker would be to try to find this right way of looking at the features of the problem. He would be made more aware of what was already implicit in what he knew. In this way the basic knowledge and expertise in a particular field could be fully utilized.

For many years physiologists could not understand the purpose of the long loops in the kidney tubules: it was assumed that the loops had no special function and were a relic of the way the kidney had evolved. Then one day an engineer looked at the loops and at once recognized that they could be part of a counter-current multiplier, a well-known engineering device for increasing the concentration of solutions. In this instance a fresh look from outside provided an answer to something that had been a puzzle for a long time. The usefulness of an outside view of a problem is not only that special experience from a different field can be brought to bear but also that the outsider is not bogged down by the particular way of approaching things that has developed in those closest to the problem. The stages by which a problem develops may commit to a particular approach someone who has been with the problem all along; someone else who has not had to follow it stage by stage, however, but sees it complete at the final state, may be able to approach it in quite a different way. The value of an outside view of things is well recognized in the use of consultants in various fields, who are expected to provide not only a superior expertise in that field but also the benefit of looking at things in a new way. Unfortunately expertise in a field does not by itself imply an ability to look at things in different ways; lateral thinking may be required for that.

Lateral thinking serves a purpose even if it acts only as a catalyst to set off some new trains of thought, some new interactions. Sometimes a new idea may be tantalizingly close to hand and yet can only come about when the final link is provided. In the same way apparently incompatible views may be found to be comparable if a particular intermediate point of view can be offered as a link.

Every decision is made with some degree of uncertainty. Confidence in a decision does not depend on the lack of any alternative, for that might only indicate lack of imagination, but on the ability to see many alternatives all of which can be rejected. In the making of any decision it can be useful to use one's own or someone else's lateral thinking to generate alternative views so that rejection of these can strengthen the decision. A free-thinking devil's advocate, instead of casting doubts on a good decision, can only succeed in strengthening it.

There is no doubt that some people are more apt to have new ideas than others. Many research departments do in fact recognize an ideas man, who is consulted whenever someone is up against a problem. Very rarely, however, is the maximum use made of ideas people. Ideas people are not usually powerful organizers; they have so many new ideas that the attraction of the latest one makes it difficult to organize the previous one. Single-mindedness, drive and determination are not characteristics of the ideas man, for he is more interested in having new ideas than in carrying them out. Ideas people do not usually organize themselves into an ideal position for having at their disposal the means to try out all their ideas. It is interesting to speculate how much of Edison's success was due to the excellent arrangement of his business interests which provided the perfect setting for his inventive genius.

People in positions of power and influence have not always got there through a facility for having new ideas. In working a way up through an orthodox organization new ideas may be more of a hindrance than an asset. Drive, energy and singlemindedness are much more effective qualities and as such are the ones rewarded. Ideas people are often accused of laziness and lack of interest, and the accusation may be perfectly valid, for a person who shows enthusiasm in the development of his own ideas may show rather less in the development of the ideas of others. James Clerk Maxwell was apparently so uninterested in ordinary school work that he was sent home as being impossible to educate. Darwin failed to get into medical school at Cambridge, and there are many other instances where a gifted mind has shown a similar lack of interest in routine learning. Unfortunately for quite a long part of his career the ideas man is used to carry out the often inferior ideas of an organizer. The usefulness of an ideas man to an organizer is reflected in the terms 'grass-hopper mind' or 'butterfly mind', which are quite fairly applied by the organizer to the ideas man who does not realize his true function. Organizers usually fail to distinguish between ideas people, of whom one needs but few, and implementers, who are the thorough and capable people who do the useful work.

Ideas people affect to despise the so-called implementers who are usually to be found working with great skill and application on second-rate ideas. What the ideas people fail to realize is that it is the implementers who really do the useful work, and without them the new ideas would be worthless. It may also be that the implementers work on second-rate ideas not because they are incapable of better ones, but because they are able to get down to work as soon as they have an idea; they are not so lazy that they require the super-inspiration of a great idea in order to get going. In the same way an implementer may work the hard way round a problem because he is capable of doing it, whereas an ideas man may have to seek out the easy way because he is too lazy or too incompetent to do it the hard way. The ideal research team would consist of an ideas man and an implementer; they would co-operate as did the architects Vanbrugh and Hawksmoor in the building of Castle Howard and Blenheim Palace.

Vanbrugh the inspired amateur provided the ideas but without the technical skill of Hawksmoor they would have come to nothing.

The days when a wealthy dilettante like Sir Humphry Davy could dabble in science are long gone. The increasing cost of technology has made it necessary to decide what ideas are to be tried out and who is to try them out. In one way or another the project or grant system has come to control research (it is difficult to see how it could be otherwise). The major drawback of the system is that the funds are administered by able administrators who are rarely ideas men, since the latter would probably not have the ability for the job. An administrator is apt to be unadventurous, particularly since he is administering someone else's money. It is preferable if the research project can be guaranteed to result in a definite outcome, for there are reports to be made and money to be accounted for. One way of ensuring a definite outcome is to back projects which have been done before and to do them again in a slightly different way: the outcome is more or less known beforehand.

A related drawback of the project system is that the proposed project must be detailed, with all its stages set out carefully. Some projects cannot be transcribed in this way. In some investigations it may be impossible to predict which way things will develop, and to state that a particular technique will be used in three years' time may not even be a good guess, let alone a fixed plan. The danger is that the closed projects get the support because they seem more real than the vague open-ended ones which depend on the development of new ideas as things go along. This problem of squaring administrative necessities with research needs is unfortunately one that can only grow more difficult.

This chapter has dealt in a general way with the use of lateral thinking and the treatment of new ideas, for the two cannot really be separated. The circumstances in which lateral thinking could be of help and the circumstances which suit lateral thinkers have been discussed. The final point that needs considering is whether there is any way of detecting the effective lateral thinkers so that they could be exploited efficiently.

By their very nature, ordinary intelligence tests would not be expected to pick out lateral thinkers. Ordinary intelligence tests are based on the way most people respond to them: a person is judged to be clever if he answers the questions in the same way as other clever people have done. In each case the right answer is the most sensible answer, the high-probability answer. But lateral thinking is concerned with low-probability answers, with seeing things in a way which no one else does. A particular example of this sort of thing is to be found in that common item in intelligence tests: the odd-man-out in a series of shapes. Very often an imaginative person can find perfectly valid reasons why a shape other than the intended one is different from the rest. Such a person is penalized for missing the correct answer, instead of getting a bonus for choosing an additional and more imaginative answer.

Tests can be devised to pick out those who might be good at lateral thinking, but they are usually tests that involve watching someone do something, observing how he tackles problems, noting his general flexibility of approach and his ability to avoid traps, rather than a standard type of question and answer.

Summary

It is possible to deal with a subject by carefully proceeding from one point to another. It is possible to describe a building by studying the architect's plans, starting first with one elevation and then going on to another, working one's way methodically over the details. But there is another way of getting to know a building, and that is to walk around it, looking at it from all sorts of different angles. Some of the views will overlap, but in the end a good general view of the building is obtained and it may turn out to be more real than that obtained by detailed study of the plans. In this book the lateral method has been used to describe the idea of lateral thinking. Instead of the neat niceties of analysis of the logical method, a succession of images and approaches has been tried in the hope that in the end a definite idea of the purpose and nature of lateral thinking may come about. A certain amount of overlapping, a certain amount of repetition, a certain amount of imprecision are inseparable from the process of bringing about an idea in this way. At this stage it may be useful to ink in a firm outline to that idea by summarizing the main point of each chapter:

Chapter 1. The difference between vertical thinking as high-probability, straight-ahead thinking, and lateral thinking as low-probability, sideways thinking.

Chapter 2. The way ideas do not, unfortunately, come about through sheer vertical effort.
Chapter 3. The polarizing effect of dominant ideas.
Chapter 4. A visual exercise in thinking.
Chapter 5. The deliberate search for the many different ways of looking at something.
Chapter 6. The arrogance of vertical thinking that prevents the emergence of new ideas.
Chapter 7. The use of chance by acknowledging its value, not interfering, encouraging chance processes, and harvesting the outcome.
Chapter 8. Illustrations of the practical use of one aspect of lateral thinking.
Chapter 9. The disadvantages of doing without lateral thinking.
Chapter 10. The exploitation of lateral thinking and the use of new ideas.

Although these chapter summaries are an attempt to divide up the subject, the same three basic themes run through all the chapters, for they are the basic themes of lateral thinking:

1. The limitations of vertical thinking as a method of generating new ideas.
2. The use of lateral processes to generate new ideas.
3. The purpose of lateral thinking to produce new ideas that are simple, sound and effective.

The techniques must, inevitably, seem very artificial, for the natural way of the mind is the vertical way. Until lateral thinking becomes habitual it can be helpful to use these artificial channels quite deliberately in order to divert the flow of ideas from the natural high-probability paths.

To my mind the charm of lateral thinking is that it is an exciting search for the simplicity of a good idea and that it is open to everyone, since it is not dependent on sheer intelligence.

The need for lateral thinking does not arise from the semantic antics of descriptive word-play, but is dictated by the functional organization of the brain which determines the pattern of thinking. These aspects will be discussed in a later work, for the first step is to examine the usefulness of lateral thinking and that is independent of its origins.

Edward de Bono

Wordpower

Could you make an *educated guess* at the *downside-risk* of a *marketing strategy*? Are you in the right *ball-game*, and faced with a *crisis* could you find an *ad hoc* solution?

These are just a few of the 265 specialized words – or 'thinking chunks' – that Dr de Bono defines here in terms of their usage to help the reader use them as tools of expression. So the next time an economic adviser talks about cash-flows, or the local councillor starts a campaign about ecology, you know what to do. Reach for *Wordpower* and add a 'thinking chunk' to your vocabulary.

Also published in Penguins

Lateral Thinking
A Textbook of Creativity

Practical Thinking
4 ways to be right;
5 ways to be wrong;
5 ways to understand

The Mechanism of Mind

Po: Beyond Yes and No

The Five-Day Course in Thinking
Introducing the L-game

Teaching Thinking

Children Solve Problems

Future Positive

The Happiness Purpose